SUPERMANSHIP
(B.4)

SUPERMANSHIP

or,

how to
continue to
STAY TOP

without actually

FALLING APART

———

by

STEPHEN POTTER

ILLUSTRATED BY LT.-COL. FRANK WILSON

RANDOM HOUSE
NEW YORK

FIRST PRINTING 1959

© Copyright, 1955, 1956, 1958, by Stephen Potter
© Copyright, 1957, by The Curtis Publishing Company
All rights reserved under International and
Pan-American Copyright Conventions.
Library of Congress Catalog Card Number: 58–10950
Printed in the United States of America

CONTENTS

CONTENTS

8

CONTENTS

PRELUDE

SIX YEARS have passed since we last issued a gamesmanship pamphlet (B.3 *One-Upmanship*). Yet these pages were the vanguard, merely, of newly co-ordinated research at the Lifemanship Correspondence College of One-Upness and Gameslifemastery.[1] Our endeavours, largely unpaid, have recently been intensified and extended to the political scene and the international sphere. These must remain secret. But feeling, naturally, that the extension of our orbit, called for a strengthening of our terminology, the introduction of a significant prefix became only a matter of time. We are no Supermen at Yeovil. But the term Supermanship, devised by our Creative Department, does convey, I hope not too pompously, the intercontinental grasp, the roots deep in human character, of what we have come to call, when we speak of the basis of our theory, The Contribution.

[1] The suffix "manship", still used by our outside workers, is generally shortened by us, now, to "'ship", or even quite frequently merely " 'p".

I

FACES OLD AND FACES NEW

 ## An Introductory Message from the Founder

("*Something of Myself*")

IT IS PLEASANT to look back. In the evening of life, or at any rate the tea-time, there are successes, and there have been things less successful.

My early volume on the great central section of Hove, wide though its field, never really sold: the history of a famous pewter-maker, a commissioned work, is not much read outside pewter circles. On the lighter side, I told the story, valuably I think, of the sudden improvement in my golf which followed my discovery of *artery-thinking*, as I called it in my manual *Down to Sixteen or Less*. (This was illustrated by action photographs of myself which I myself actually took, by means of a simple device of ordinary pulleys and a piece of ordinary tape.) But there are plenty left of the first printing.[1]

[1] During the war, I wrote for the B.B.C.'s Overseas wavelength a series aimed at the strengthening of morale—really dramatised

13

And then the queer accident. Philosophy I would have chosen, but the public must decide otherwise. I browse in the realms of Behaviouristicism and Implied Anthropology, and behold the result. Gamesmanship and Lifemanship have had followers, though not always the ones I expected. And when an alert student pointed out to me the other day that it was now twenty-five years since the incident of "Joad's Request", as it has come to be called—since the day, that is, when Joad called across the lawn tennis court the words "kindly say clearly, please, whether the ball is in or out" [1]—it seemed to all of us that notice should be taken, an occasion marked.

There was nothing sentimental—no "gush". One of the nicest things for me was that a special Lifemanship Literary Luncheon was organised for me by Miss Ivy Spring, Yeovil's sole female staffer. The small tables for onlookers were only partially filled (the date clashed by chance with the arrival of the Brazilian Commission) but the "high" table was full of guests distinguished in many walks of life and included F. C. Littleman, the famous anthologist of bowls and (friend from the past) Anne Briar, water-

biographies of British and Dominion writers—Pope and Peacock, Blake, Milton and the rest. These were twenty minutes apiece, and well packed moreover with material showing the first struggles, early conflicts, later struggles, and last struggles—there was scarcely a line of dialogue which was not the result of reading and research. I printed a collection, adding my suggestions for background music, most of it from Elgar and Brahms. But *Airborne Heritage* sold, I think, less well than any of them.

[1] See *Gamesmanship*, p. 17.

colourist of broadcasting fame. We much enjoyed the *bons vins* and dishes provided by the *chef maître* of the Clapham Junction Hotel.[1]

CARRYING ON

Work is constantly in progress at Yeovil, though little of it sees the light of day. Only last month a stranger wrote asking for news in enthusiastic terms —though by the way it irritates me if my first name is spelt with a v. We have continued to keep ourselves free of the old pernicious educational strangleholds of "test" and examination. Our diplomas, by no means expensive to buy, must, though, be signed by at least *one* other member of our staff besides myself.[2] If the I.Q. of our students is low, it is because we are keeping it so—because it is not in the parrot-like ability to write down the correct answers, in the unpleasant precocity which enables the student to be at his best in, of all places, the examination room, that we place our faith. Mere written work is on the whole discarded. We teach our students to make, to act—to "get their hands dirty" as we say, and they succeed in this extraordinarily well.

Apropos, a question from Oxford! "Yes, but how do you do that with the young economist?" asked once of me shyly R. Harrod, of Ch.Ch.

---

[1] Gattling-Fenn, the only member to make two speeches, gave me a clock, with a plate inset for an inscription (he insisted that if I chose the wording I could have it done myself). Odoreida gave me a very useful little upkeep set for my spectacles.

[2] This other member must never be G. Odoreida.

WE ALSO HELD . . .

... A LIFEMANSHIP RALLY

17

"By sending him into the coalmines, instead of bemusing him with fuel figures or supply and demand curves. By putting him into grubby overalls, to pick up a lump and question the miner, eager to teach him, on the spot. A month in a drawing-pin factory bringing cups of tea to the men who mix nickel with brass is worth six months' study of the inverse demand curves of international alloys. Later we teach them to make real graphs out of pieces of wire; and the squared paper is ruled by a group of pretty dark-haired girls."

Faces Old . . .

Gattling-Fenn and the rest are still with us, needless to say, at the prime of whatever age they are. "Rattling Gattling" as we call him, Gattling the bit of a cadman, is still forceful and eager. After twenty-five years of being the oldest young man at Yeovil, he has now entered into a new lease of life as the youngest old one. When, in the summer, he addresses, in the open air, a small group of students sitting out of doors relaxed on the natural asphalt, he now concentrates on being amazing for his age. Owing to his exercises, which we hear something of before breakfast, he is definitely able to sit springily on his heels. He never now changes from the blazer and Old Wantage scarf which he wore on the occasion when he first applied for his post with us.

Cogg-Willoughby is now the internationally accepted scholar of Gameslife and spends his time codifying and rectifying. Every day through the Wild Garden between the roller and the greenhouse, both out of use, he delicately picks his way for twenty minutes and it is generally recognised that this is Cogg's relaxation, and no student is allowed, or wants, to speak to him.

G. Odoreida is still—Odoreida. He holds no actual Lectureship with us and has not for four years. We did allow him, when he advertised for pupils, to refer to himself as "sometime Reader at the Lifemanship College": but by altering "sometime" to "sometimes," he managed to give the impression that he occasionally did us a good turn, and that it was he who had parted with us, instead of vice-versa.

In fact, for the moment—doubtless a very brief one—Odoreida is enjoying an extraordinary success. His evening seminars at home are really well attended —quite enough to fill the hateful little study of "Wendyways." He actually pretends to be selecting applicants, making students on their first appearance pore over intelligence-tests cribbed from job-suitability tests and of course quite beyond Odoreida, who scribbles "neater work" or "very fair" or "mind sp." at random on the top of some wooden hexagon, cut-out triangle of newspaper, or some other mysterious Test object completely incomprehensible to him.

Wert of our staff is returned to us. In my absence he was somehow "cleared" of the charge of Unlifemanlike Activities. I mention him now because it was he who discovered an extraordinarily irritating thing about Odoreida; which was that in his private seminars he actually charges 15/6 for a half-hour of "instruction," during which of course he teaches those ploys and gambits of that very kind which we always try to keep out of the clean and straightforward atmosphere of Yeovil. Gattling was particularly angry and once said to him in front of a student: "How on earth do you get away with it, charging fifteen and six?"

I knew what Odoreida's answer would be. It was a ploy he was very keen on at that time. He stuck his little head against the back of his armchair, looked at the ceiling mildly, and held his arms out straight, palms down.

"I.T." he said in a sing-song voice to the tune of the first two notes of the *War Song of the Priests*. "Income Tax, my dear," he continued to the girl, who annoyingly enough had rather elaborate dark eyes, and had been heard to refer to Odoreida as "podge." Money of any sort only had to be mentioned in any kind of big way for Odoreida to look at his finger-nails and say "I.T."

"Fifteen and six is exactly fivepence three farthings after deduction."

Gattling was much too annoyed to answer, though he later got Ivy Spring to work out what Odoreida's income would have to be if this remark were true. Answer: £216,750 p.a.

OUR NEW H.Q. (This drawing was executed before the repairs to the left section of the outside wall were put into full operation.)

. . . and Faces New

But now for our big bit of news. What of the College Building itself, you will say? Is it true that it has been taken over by the National Trust? No. It has of course been visited unofficially by students of its particular periods, 1876 and 1891, which have been the subject of an article in our Journal by L. Brice and Veronica P. Hartridge; of the very few bricks of the original wall in the front garden which have been disturbed, all have been put back in the same order. Whether or not it will eventually be bought for the National Trust we want to know quickly: because the big news is that we have moved our headquarters from 681 Station Road to a new superheadquarters No. 675, just the other side of the level-crossing.

This was an important decision for us. The new building is actually smaller, but it is infinitely preferable because it is infinitely more modern. In period houses such as 681, it is true, students drink in an enormous amount of history through the pores, even if they don't know the date of Trafalgar. But how much more in key with the new Lifemanship is 675. Totally untraditional, it is sheathed in concrete while one whole big side of it is half glass, or looks vaguely like it. Look at it from Siemann's the tobacconists and see how colour and atmosphere are given by reflection only, in the glass sheeting, of signals and telegraph poles, tautly upright, and as counterpoint the yellow smoke-plumes from the engine-funnels. Indoors you can say the atmosphere is controlled. The roof is wide open to the sun, and there are days when definite sun-bathing is possible, which will be more generally enjoyed when our plea for smokeless fuel in Essential Products Ltd., our nearby factory, has met with some response, or our letter is at any rate answered. The whole thing was created by Tackton in 1925 and partly derives from the Chapel of the Secondary School at Ausvierfleischenhültz. The window frames are by Slipton, the chimneys by Skipton, and the filling material, used to cover the cracks formed by the rather lovely weathering to which all concrete is subject, is by Odzon.

The new grounds are smaller too, but what do we have instead of the old-fashioned garden? An outdoor museum, a gallery open to sky and wind, of

A CORNER OF OUR NEW COMMON ROOM.

Gameslife mementoes. Over there is the original internal-combustion engine with the device for starting the car from under the bonnet, invented by Godfrey Plaste to give the impression of mechanical aptitude; and close by, the actual processed cheese advertisement taken from the wall of Aldgate East Underground Station at the exact point where the Founder first thought of Potter's Opening at Chess. By the gate, the dusky white of a patch of viscid sneezewort has sown itself, gentle visitor, in our grounds.

C. Sticking

C. STICKING.

We were enormously helped in our decision to move, and in our choice of a home, by a welcome addition to our staff who must now be introduced. For a long time we had had the feeling that the atmosphere needed modernising: and Cornelius—"Corny" —Sticking was obviously the man. He was easy and big and wore thick sports coats. "Such a wonderfully unfrightened head," Effie Weeks said: and it was Gattling who pointed out that his up-to-dateness was proved by his courageous way of breaking fetters, even on buses or at tea time. Indeed he broke fetters on holiday, as I remembered on a week-end at the Maudesleys. The house was in the rather densely kitchen-farmed and thickly populated area of mid-Essex, and I always remember my introduction to a Sticking "country walk". No sooner did we get onto a road or even a path than he leapt or grubbed his way through a hedge in order to continue in a straight line if possible. This took much longer, but S. insisted on this straight line because he wanted to treat this chewed-over part of Essex as if it was as wild and empty

24

as Winnipeg prairie, walking indiscriminately across back gardens, small fields made of a kind of glue, and the winter parking-quarters of caravanettes. How he enjoyed it—but what? He was completely blind to the quite pretty water-colour landscape, though he did once refer—at the world record unsuitable moment, I should have said—to something being "typical Constable". The whole point of his walks was this smashing through in big boots past NO ENTRY notices and anti-trespasser signs. And it took me quite a long time before I realised that when Sticking plunged straight across the corner of Mr. Butts's orchard, disturbing the chickens, what he was saying was "the land is for the people", as if in some way he was more people than old Mr. Butts.

What was the secret of the Sticking gambit? For although in the end Cannery and the Other Man between them got Sticking down, we certainly learnt a lot from his basic approach.

The simplicity of Sticking's primary attack is what makes it so difficult to counter. In a way, it is simply a laugh, simply Sticking's laugh, big and Falstaffian, blowing away cobwebs. A happy, guilt-free laugh—"gloriously sane", little Effie Weeks called it.[1] Sometimes he went too far: but it was extraordinarily difficult to counter.

[1] It could make people simply ache with indignation. "What, frighted with false fires?" he would say to a brilliant young art critic who said that except for the Meistersingers he wasn't very keen on Wagner. "He's worth a hundred of these jazz saxophonists." There was something so absolutely inappropriate, on five levels simultaneously, about "jazz saxophonists," that it seemed hopeless even to try to answer back.

The Coming of the Lawrenceman

Or so, for a long time, we thought.

Sticking ruled the roost, with his wonderful gambit of driving home the out-of-dateness of a date so distant that most of his audience had never even heard of it. The Founder apart, Sticking for about fourteen months was top man in the lifeplay: and he was destined to play a useful part long after that. But after the coming of the Lawrenceman, his major power was gone.

When exactly did this tremendously new face first appear? There was this boy, my second cousin Ginger. He was playing Red Indians in a wood and "found a funny man with a beard" who said, according to an observer, that "the cool prying of the North child can never find the secret of Poplihotl." This was the Lawrenceman. He was small, pale, intent, serious, with rather large plastic features in a small face, and a big dark beard, round and soft and soggy. The shadows on his face made me think, when I first saw him, that he was standing under a gas lamp, but of course he wasn't. When he spoke, which was seldom, it was in an undertone. Mrs. Fenn, who rather liked him, said he had a very sensitive mouth, and everybody wondered

THE LAWRENCEMAN

26

how she had seen it, under this poultice of beard and hair. Whether he had ever actually read the works of D. H. Lawrence we could never prove; but he did look like a warmed-up version of this great man and he did get hold of a few phrases and he made good use of them. It took a long time, but under the Lawrenceman treatment Sticking's confidence began to seep away. I first noticed it when Sticking was in one of his disgusted moods being disgusted about some Somerset people, who "put on their best clothes to go to morning service on Sundays". "Is that a badness?" said the Lawrenceman mildly. Stickers froze.

"Your question?" said Stickers, pretty crisp.

"I think it has something of good, or is a symbol of something good." You would never guess that the voice came from the motionless beard of the Lawrenceman.

"Remarkably little to do with Christianity," said Sticking. I felt we were in for a dose of Golden Bough, but somehow the Lawrenceman checked him.

"Perhaps," he said. There was something tip-top about the placid way this word was said. He went on:

"Yet there is a ceremony of departure, a sacrifice. On the hill they lit the wood fire to the morning." Lawrenceman's eyes were wide open, but he wasn't looking at anybody.

"You don't make yourself clear," said Sticking, in his most distinct voice.

"Can anybody *make* themselves clear?" Lawrenceman turned to Sticking for the first time.

"That is the general supposition."

"I think a man can make his words clear, and even his thoughts. But himself . . .?" After this stunning and really first-class statement, Lawrence-man turned his back on us and walked to the window, and Sticking made a mistake. He tried to *look* clear. We realised even then that it was a beginning, and a portent. People began to say "Poor Sticking." For after all he was on the right side in the right arguments. He was a good Wolfenden man, a first-class don't say "don't" to children man. But even if he said something fairly unarguable, as he often did, sometimes overdoing it in fact, repeating for instance that the long-range H-bomb was madness, the Lawrenceman could somehow get him down with Slow Withdrawn Look and use some all-round-the-compass phrase like "Does then the destroyer hate the destroyer?" Sticking would bury himself in a nest of galley proof. After about twelve minutes he would get up and walk in a markedly open-air way to the Railway Station Buffet and order a small stout. "You can't argue with a fog," he said, "or a marsh mallow." But he never did get round to answering back the Lawrenceman, so in the end Sticking was forced to change places with him, officially, on the Lifemanship ladder.

The Mild Young Men and I. Cannery

For a long time it looked as if the Lawrenceman was to master us all. Of course I always knew what the counter to him was, but I wanted staff and students alike to find it out for themselves: besides I liked Lawrenceman, and wanted him to have his day. The end came simply and naturally, with yet one more new member of the staff, who in his simple manner was the master not only of Sticking but of Lawrenceman as well. It happened in rather a curious way.

Dealing with correspondence is always a problem. A whole bundle of letters was on our desk three years ago asking us What is the attitude of Yeovil to the Angry Young Man?

In fact Yeovil as a whole did not care for this movement, since most of us, about thirty-three years ago on the average, had been angry young men ourselves, in fact much angrier, and this particular movement of our own had attracted no attention

MILD YOUNG MEN
(The candidates' waiting-room at Yeovil has never before been shown to Anyone.)

whatever. We took the obvious step of trying to engage, countering, an exceptionally mild young man for our staff, and I well remember the millions of cups of tea we had, interviewing candidates for this post, and the feeling as if one was trying to play squash rackets in a court whose walls were made of semolina pudding, when in answer to our hundredth impatient question, the fifteenth candidate said: "Ah, but I see good in that too."

In the end, as is well known, the post was allotted to the candidate who was easily the best mild young man we saw: the only fault, if a fault, being that he was not exceptionally young. That is how we got Irwin Cannery.

We all liked Cannery, at first, anyhow. Not only was he mild, he was nice, and in spite of his mildness he was tremendously enthusiastic about his subject, which was the history of lift styles. That is how he got the Lawrenceman.

At first we were flattered by his interest in our old Yeovil H.Q. No. 681. "Perfect 1892 . . . 1892 dead centre," he said, literally rubbing his nose into the plaster work over the bell-push. But the amazing thing was that he subjected our fine modern concrete building to exactly the same treatment. "Debased Bodzinsky," he said, looking at our roof from the little sweetshop on the

I. CANNERY.

other side of the road. "Delightfully wrong here. 1932 exactly." Actually it was 1931, but we had to admire him—especially when he took exactly the same line with Sticking, as if Sticking was debased Bodzinsky too.

"Surely this is superior to your aspidistra and lace curtains," Sticking said, progressively, pointing to a cactus on the window-sill.

"A-*ha*!"

Cannery turned on him a rapturously period-spotting eye.

"Aha, don't tell me you've got the complete works of Sidney and Beatrice Webb," he said.

"No, I have not." Sticking was pretty brusque. He was getting fed up with some aspects of his life at Yeovil.

"Ah, but how about *Progress and Poverty*? No . . . that wouldn't be right . . . *The Intelligent Woman's Guide to Socialism*?" Cannery added intently.

"I suppose you don't approve of such works," said Sticking, tentatively sheltering behind his basic gambit.

"Approve? I *adore* them," said Cannery. "And now about your name? Sticking? Isn't it actually a place-name in Essex? Essex would be too perfect, *too* Shawsy-Wellsy, isn't it."

Sticking had a good idea. Pretending that he thought Cannery was really asking a question, he said: "Perhaps the Lawrenceman can tell you."

Lawrenceman was delicately putting a log on the fire, and watching the mystery of the smoke.

"Come on," said Sticking, "What do *you* make of Irvin Cannery?"

Lawrenceman didn't look up. "I cannot 'make' a man, I hope. If I could I would ask, when he enjoyed the fruits, the outerworks, why he did not let himself comprehend—know—the roots."

"A-HAA!" Cannery turned on Lawrenceman more delighted than ever. "I *love* you. Are you really a Blake man! So am I! And I bet you don't think much of Bertrand Russell."

Then Cannery asked him a dozen questions, trying to place Lawrenceman, who became, in fact, more and more silent. Later on our three new members, Sticking, the Lawrenceman and Cannery, used to sit round countering and cross-countering each other. "Progress," said Sticking in effect: "In what sense . . ." said the Lawrenceman: "Period," said Cannery, "it's dead right, for period." Cannery always seemed to get the last word.

So much for our staff and headquarters. The pages which follow are a record of work accomplished, of researches in Supermanship.

At the beginning, the simple things; not less bold because the subjects are familiar.

II

YEOVIL JUBILEE PAMPHLETS

General Domestic and Sociological Problems with Special Reference to Inter-Family Superbehaviourism.

1. SUPERBABY

The Baby as Lifeman

Children! What a vast subject. Superchild is in all our lives: and in pamphlet and essay, many of them printed in earlier volumes, we have dealt with them, though not finally.

There still remains to be discussed, however, that much more important gambit-field, the infant or newborn baby. And let me say at once that we of L.C.C. are against the ugly pictures, often showing them as debased ruffians, of our English children as drawn by many of our "comic" artists today. It has been proved that in their facies, or general appearance, 53% of the newly-born seem acceptable to their parents.

Indeed it is clear that babies are by nature one-up. Whatever they do it is your fault and your fault only. Babies cannot be, and are not supposed to be, good, reasonable or considerate. Further, they are completely unsusceptible to the normal life-attacks.

The grieved look means nothing to them; the firm tone is something they know how to deal with. It is no good turning away from them with a supercilious curl of the lip. They cannot be patronised. Their reaction to such remarks as "There's a clever little boy" is a long stare in the opposite direction.

Pre-Natal Lull

The target of Superbaby's gambits is its parents. During the pre-natal period the parents have a feeling of invulnerability, of being in charge. It is their conviction that they "have decided to have it". It is a hushed, O.K. period of "baby's on the way", with very few premonitions at first of the fact that from the point of view of the approaching lifewave it is "parents on the way", that it is you, the parent, who are about to meet for the first time the full shock of living. "Of course I'm still playing tennis" is the brave, pathetic last flutter of the parental flag.

"We timed it so that we could go to Cornwall as usual." Inside, gruff and grim is ominously silent.

Nevertheless, though between conception and birth parents may have an uneasy sensation that they are about to be taken charge of, yet there is no doubt that at first the mother is in a fine lifeposition, and even begins getting fond of the baby in anticipation.[1]

Indeed, the woman is a heroine and knows it.

[1] Corny Sticking will wave his wet blanket even at this early stage, taking the anthropological approach, common-sensing right and left, and pointing out that the whole thing is as instinctive as an ants' nest and that it's simply due to millions of years of evolution, because mammals started as far back as Late Chalk.

Certain fathers, as is well known, try to suggest that they are fairly heroic also. In fact at the other end of the scale, in the slums and dingy café society of borderlifemanship, there are some husbands who have succeeded in suggesting that it is they who need special attention, the extra drink brought to them, the cushion carried from another room for the small of *their* back. No one will be surprised to learn that Odoreida, for instance, during the last three months of his wife's pregnancy, used to take every opportunity of sitting down in a collapsed sort of way and getting people to pass him things. In golf, if the match was going against him, he would walk in after the fourteenth, two down and four to play, "because his muscles seemed to have lost all give." And any time from seven months to go till two days before it was supposed to happen (when he should have been at home anyhow) Odoreida used to anger us (while gaining kudos from those who did not know him) by a "half a minute" exit after the sixteenth hole, which

ODOREIDA "TELEPHONING"

happens to be near our clubhouse, "to ring home".

"I shan't be happy unless I know she's all right", he would say. "I think she'd rather like to hear the sound of my voice."

We often had to wave through two singles and a fourball before he joined us: and the maddening thing is that I was never so placed as to be able to prove what I was inwardly certain of—that he never went near the telephone, but was simply standing and drinking, quite slowly, two Scotch and sodas.

The Primordial Protoployic Gambule[1]

But in truth the expectant parents are proud and happy people. Getting them down is no easy matter. Yet notice the powerful simplicity of the baby, the first act in whose life is a ploy.

He cries—to attract attention. But note—it is not just a call: apparently it is weeping. Imitation, you will say. Fake. But there are sobs, and a special kind of retractable tear. Yet when picked up the baby is relaxed, contented and thinking of something else; and quite often this big blob of tear has gone altogether, as if sucked back into the eye. This is no reasoned and deliberate plan—far deadlier, it is the result of instinctive lifemanship, at its purest and most powerful. That the instinct goes very deep is obvious in the many ways in which the baby can keep its parents and general entourage dangling on the wires. The skilled superbaby by a collapsed

[1] Gambule. A new word for Gambit, it means precisely the same thing. Its use depends on usage—e.g. I am writing it here.

motion of the shoulders, for instance, and a swivel-
lingly swerving motion of the neck, can suggest that
its head is loose. A cunning baby can do this
especially during those inter-suck pauses when the
bottle is laid aside and the sun stops still in the heavens
because the child is supposed to burp. The good
burpman can keep a room full of friends, relations
and causal business acquaintances in rigid and
unnatural silence for perhaps a minute till the burp
comes. Everybody's position becomes fixed as if
they were listening to the reading of a will. More
deeply instinctive is the power to come out in a rash
all over the scalp which, after the father has stood
twenty minutes in a queue for a special baby oint-
ment only to find that he has to go back to the
doctor for a prescription, disappears completely one
minute before he gets home. Some babies are able, in
the cot, to seem to be breathing at three times the
normal rate; others to be showing no sign of life
whatsoever, so that they have to be taken up to
make sure they are not stone-dead: others specialise
in bizarre and puzzling symptoms which vanish
completely while the doctor, urgently summoned,
is actually ringing the door-bell, so that in time the
doctor decides he is being hoaxed and refuses to
come even when there is genuine cause to suspect
scarlet fever. By practising some form of rigidity on
the scales a few are able to show "no increase"; but
be sure that on the more expensive scales of Harley
Street the weight will be exactly and completely
average.

37

Besides this anxiety play of new-born infants, which is simple and strong, they have a set of effective little ploys which may be described as *Wrong Mood.* If its pretty and fastidious godmother is coming to see it in the afternoon, it will scratch its nose in the norning so that all she sees is a long diagonal scab. When she gives a gift—a valuable heirloom rattle, for instance—superbaby will get red on one side of its face only, go icy cold in the left hand, and eat the brown paper the thing was wrapped up in.

The Attack from Outside

Not only the baby itself, but external forces will soon be concentrated on the undermining of the parents. Baby Literature makes itself felt first, and Baby Instruction. Many prettily got-up booklets start with the dictum "Enjoy Your Baby".[1] This approach does well by repeating, first, that having a baby is as natural and jolly as a visit to the old Victoria Music Hall, and then going into very small print with graphs, diet charts, and measurements in "c.c.".

Yet the "c.c." part of it is less dampening than the last section of the book, which always recommends that the baby should be surrounded by beautiful things, and beautiful sounds. Gattling-Fenn, the only time he stayed with us, made this an excuse for playing the piano, which we never normally allowed him to do. Every day he played a sort of psalmified

[1] Known at Yeovil as the Petrification of the Implied Opposite.

version, with hymny chords, of "Once you have found her Never let her go," because, he said, the piano was just over the nursery.

Many of one's friends develop attacking gambits suitable to the baby situation. I quite admired Cannery's contribution, though it takes time and trouble. It is a well-known fact that some fathers are rather clumsy about handling their own babies, especially their first babies, and pick them up as if they were made of pastry. They curve both arms underneath them, bowing low so that the babies have less far to fall if dropped; and if they walk it is with a wide-apart bow-legged gait to avoid tripping up. The baby cries. It was Cannery who had the good idea of learning this one thing, this lifting of babies. He had observed exactly the technique of one great clothes-horse of a monthly nurse who treated the baby as if it was a punch ball, humped it over while she was washing it as if she was basting a leg of mutton, shoved the bottle into its mouth like a dentist's gag, and could lift it up a circular staircase carrying a towel, a waste-paper basket and a bottle of disinfectant at the same time. It was this grip which Cannery practised. When some mother said "Would you like to take him for just one second?" she would be horrified and then admiring to see him take hold of the baby with his safety lock on the child's thigh and swing it round in a way which gave satisfaction everywhere. "It's always been instinctive with me," he would say, holding the baby upside down.

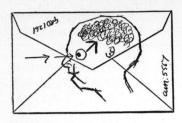

DIAGRAM BY ZIMMERS.

Demonstrating that "Look, I think he recognised you," must be nonsense, unless the association centres of the infant brain (marked in fuzzy lines) are abnormally developed or hypertrophied.

Another Friend approach is exemplified by Zimmermann. As everybody knows, Zimmermann is Sticking's younger brother. Quite early in life he changed from Sticking to Zimmermann in the belief that this name was much more suitable for a research anthropologist. He is also, and here I rather envy him, one of those excellently lifeplaced individuals who have a degree in Medicine yet do something else. Surely it was worth it, this going to Port Despair University, off the coast of Greenland, Disko Island, where medical degrees are rather simple to get, in order to become M.D. and do something else. The something else he used to be an expert in varied, but with babies it was always anthropology.

"Well, who do you think he is like?" we would ask him—a fatal question when Zimmers is around because after talking about the "factor of changing appearance in the newly born" he would scribble inheritance diagrams on the baby's weight chart proving that so far from taking after its parents, it was only by the merest stroke of luck that the baby, if a boy, was still alive. Zimmers could then pass easily to the sterilised approach, making you feel, in spite of all your nursery scrubbing and boiling, that the baby might as well be eating off the farmyard floor. Or he would switch to raised eyebrows at the diet. "Nowadays we are giving them the equivalent of sardines on toast by week nine." I must say that without being a complete cad that old Ph.D. left us as miserable as most. He did not actually cast doubts on the suitability of our doctor. I believe he once tried that on Odoreida who, I am bound to say, did well by asking, in the same tone of voice, who had been the doctor at Zimmers's birth and pretending to be very interested because Zimmers couldn't answer.

Is There a Counter?

There is no doubt that there are parents capable of answering back. Some mothers have a kind of school-matron approach with visitors, telling them not to smoke, not to leave the door open, not to make sudden noises or movements, not to crackle paper, not to greet or touch the child, not to be ingratiating, and not, above all, to breathe in the infant's face. Mrs. Coad-Sanderson had some fine successes with this kind of toughness and once kept three brothers-in-law, all regular soldiers (gunners) —one a brigadier—in sterilised face-masks for nearly ninety minutes—men who had turned up under the impression that by coming to see her baby they were doing a nice thing.

But, in general, once the child is born, the Life-manship Force in array against the parent is strong,

our techniques well studied and pursued unflinch-
ingly. At the same time we are scientists and are
equally glad to record, for the pleasure of adding
one more brick to the pyramid of objective truth,
that so far as discouraging parents from having
children is concerned, our work has had no result
of any kind whatsoever.

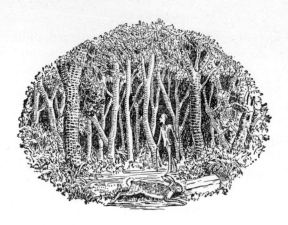

2. THE GREAT VICE VERSA
(*Town versus Country*)[1]

This primordial lifetheme has never yet been officially dealt with by us. Why? Because the opportunities for blast and counterblast are too dangerous; the one-downness of the subtended situation too potential. It is only after anxious discussion with a Ruridecane of York that we put forward this emasculated account of techniques permissible under this head. It has always been, and is here I hope, our aim to present our approach in terms deemed wise for family reading.

What is this about? A major proportion of English people belong to one of two camps, Town or Country. Your home may be in what you are not naturally one of. There are small groups perhaps who, in the

[1] These primary strictures were worked out by the Founder, F. Wilson, and the Leading Lifewoman. Surely the fact that their material was made use of is sufficient reward and acknowledgement. Any talk of "two bob per point used" would be as ungracious as it is out of place.

pursuit of supertaxmanship, have a foothold in each. But none of these modifications affects the primary type.

In order to disguise[1] the two contrasted characters we have in mind, we will call them Willie Westover and Edward Brick. Willie is Supercountry: Supertown is Edward.

Supertown in Supercountry

This is the basic situation: Town spends weekend with Country. Edward, Town, has strong feeling that on not less than seven week-ends a year, he should leave his three rooms in Albany—he comes, fourth generation, from a strain of primitive flat-dwellers—and take the 4.10 east from Liverpool Street to Old Soking. He will enjoy the very smokiness of Liverpool Street; "4.10" has a magic, the waiting room of Mark's Tey Station is faery. He will arrive in a state of mild happiness, a placid expectation, even a pleasure in Englishness not seriously scarred by the necessity of reading the *New Statesman*, which he had read up to the end of 'This Way Madness Lies' anyhow before reaching Ingatestone.

This sleepy contentment is precisely the state of mind which it is the business of Willie, Supercountry, to undermine. Willie will meet Edward, of course; but the train has moved off before Edward spots him waving over his shoulder from the other end of the platform. His back to Edward, who has two heavy bags, Willie is talking hard to the station master,

[1] Disguised against their will. But we are against giving publicity.

W. WESTOVER (*right*) GREETS E. BRICK (*left*)
This record has been carefully drawn to demonstrate the Westover
Wave, or minimum effusive greeting.

complimenting him on having won second prize for
growing the best vegetable garden on the Yeldham
branch line. He takes Edward's new bag in strong
grasp which strains handle. "Good old Edward," he
says. "Coming to pieces in several places at once."

This is a good beginning because in fact it is
Willie who is inclined to break apart: Edward never.
Willie then pushes Edward into a Land Rover, first
leaving Edward's white doeskin suitcase on the
bonnet, thus giving it its first dose of bat-droppings.
The back of the car is full of vague shapes, and there
is a bundle reducing space in front, which means that
Edward has to shut up like a jack-knife in order to
get in. [1]

Edward will make mental note that next time it

---

[1] Edward guesses that the "something" includes a large black sack,
which occasionally moves slightly, and which he will have to help
carry out: he is aware that there will be no drink.

45

will be better, on the whole, to do the old dreary beat by car past Seven Sisters on to that kaleidoscope of gay scenery, A12, via Hangman's Corner and three single-line traffic-queues in the Brentwood area.[2]

The actual fifth-class track which Willie calls The Drive has a well made exhaust-winkler—i.e. a bump which claws off the silencer of any car less effectively high-slung than Willie's Land Rover. Willie then will make a tremendous point of having cleared out his "bere-wick" (Willie must on no account be allowed to enlarge derivationally about the meaning of this word). However hard Edward will have made up his mind, driving down, to keep his new and glistening saloon away from one of Willie's "garages" he will feel obliged to back the car to Willie's "left hand hard down—no hard" routine, (specially simplified for Londoner) so that it is inevitably buried in the straw and sacking at the back, because Willie is absolutely determined that the door of this barn must shut, so that Edward's car (which Willie always refers to as "the hearse") will be placed centrally beneath the nameless exudations, the bird and bat refuse, and the splashes of an acid substance which leave a stain long after the car has returned from its special cleaning.

[2] If Edward asks Willie to send him full directions somehow distinguishing which of the dozen *steep dip down to white gate, advise you approach it in first, and please shut gate again after you* it is which actually marks the gap leading to Willie's house, Willie will respond to this request warmly, sending sketch maps with quaint little jokes on them—e.g. "here is Brick's Folly" (where Edward once twisted ankle) . . . "Wood. Wylde beasties here." The plan has twenty roads going off into nothing and is unorientated.

As Edward clambers out over piles of pig-food his host warns him when he gets to the threshold: "Sorry, we have a silly rule here. Shoes off. Brings mud in."

If Supercountry's house happens to be large, enormous sections of it, the best, will be shut off and unheated. "We only open these up when we have to put on our best bib and tucker." If by any chance these unopened rooms have any kind of architectural merit, or are remotely Adam in design, or have more than a three-line mention in an *Ancient Monuments*, wife of host will early on cold morning ask guest his advice about moving furniture because "Otto Carling is coming down, and I'm terrified of what he'll say. I hope you don't think William and Mary looks absurd in this little alcove". The point of this question is to take no notice of guest's answer.

The undermining of guest's confidence by references to past and future guests whom "we feel rather frightened of," was a gambit also employed by Willie Westover: and it must be said that he did well with his One Meal version of the Chief Guest approach. Willie would arrange the week-end meals so that they were exceptionally scratch and sardinified except for one, the Saturday luncheon, preparations for which, with full discussions, will have been apparently going on since mid-week. By Saturday morning every member of the household, including the usual guest (according to Edward, who was this "ordinary" guest) is called into the kitchen to do amusing jobs, especially grinding or

47

cutting things into very small pieces. By 11.30 there is a break for "elevenses for the lunch workers".[1] At 11.55 Willie blows a trumpet and puts on a chef's hat for some extraordinary sauce which is then put on the stove, and such a *pièce-de-résistance* atmosphere is built up round this sauce that Edward's spirits droop and dwindle at the thought of the congratulations and jokey French which will have to be dragged out for the "success," when it is eventually served, of this sauce, the miraculous point of which will be that it contains some unheard of ingredient like hawthorn-leaf wine, the local name of which is cockroach claret.

"And then, and *then* who do you think the guest was after all this?" No need to ask me that question. "Otto Carling, the Horrible."[2]

"And how does O.C. do it?" What is the secret? For those interested in the Carling angle on this—for it wasn't only at the Willie Westovers that he managed to extract these specially prepared lunches —I can reveal Carling's method. It is to make absolutely no comment on the food, to be completely silent about the wine, and especially to say nothing whatever about the sauce. And never, under any circumstances, to say Thank You.

Of all Willie's gambits this one of the Special Guest was the one which Edward found most

[1] This, according to Edward, is the first decent meal of the week-end.

[2] Carling was best known as the man who had diddled Meat Marketing Board in 1944, did a special trade in clothing coupons, and published a book illustrated by his own woodcuts on My Fayre Sussex.

difficult to endure. It is not necessary to say that with his very long nose and shapeless figure Carling had no vestige of charm nor goodness of looks; and this made his triumph all the more exasperating. Edward had ways of countering, as we shall see later. In the very throes of this luncheon he would amuse himself by planning a cocktail party in his Albany flat which he would arrange "specially for Willie", when Willie came to visit. The carefully selected guests, quite well-known in a slightly suspect way which would nevertheless appeal to Willie—the compère of Willie's favourite T.V. panel game, perhaps. While Willie was filling up Carling's glass, at least two and half times to every once for Edward, Edward would plan exactly how when Willie came bursting in to meet all these "famous coves of yours", Willie would find himself stuck in a corner with Edward's aunt and never get nearer to Panel Game, or Everest as Far as Camp Four, than Edward's purposely generalised and untruthful "You know everybody here don't you".

On a cold Sunday morning, if Edward had put on a good but thin tweed suit, Willie would pat him chaffingly on the back, say he "could see Edward was not a countryman" and take him out for a good walk, or perhaps simply to the church along a muddy "short cut," lending Edward a pair of galoshes which were much too big for him and which kept sucking off. Edward would certainly be taken to church if Willie knew it was his turn to be sidesman. He would pass the plate personally to

Edward, putting a new pound note in himself. Although Edward was practically certain that Willie would take this pound note out again afterwards, he felt constrained to look impersonal and fish for his only ten bob note, which would be scrunched up.

All this was not unsubtle on Willie's part, as it prepared for the visit to the pub between church and lunch. This was bound to be the low moment of Edward's day anyhow because the only drink available was pints of tremendously watered beer, any possible core of alcoholic content of which could not conceivably be retained in the body long enough to take effect.[1]

The object of the pound note ploy was to leave Edward short of money so that Edward embarrassingly could not stand his round of six pints. Needless to say Willie made the most of this business of standing Edward's round for him.

"Nonsense," he would say, "You're my guest from the very moment you set foot inside Hollyhock Lodge".

Edward would quite have liked to have talked to one or two of the nice old men with amusing faces in this pub, and it seemed to him that quite a few of them weren't too mad on Willie Westover. But as soon as Edward made a move in their direction Willie would pull him aside by the elbow and in a

[1] The alternative was a sherry, dark purple in colour, the taste of which rather pleasantly reminded Edward of the days when, kneeling in church in prayer at the age of six, he used to suck the varnish off the back of the pew in front.

sort of roaring whisper ask him "why he didn't speak to them".

"Talk to them. Mix with them. Old Cracky over there" —Willie would point a stubby finger at a man in the corner whose head was sunk so low that Edward could see a little way down his back.

"Old Cracky——"

Hearing what he knew Willie supposed to be his name, Cracky slowly turned his eyes, one yellow and one red, in their direction.

"Old Cracky, now he is a *real* person."[1]

Counter-country

Many were the little counterplots and plans we discussed with Edward when he returned dim and baffled from a week with Supercountry. What to do with Willie on his return visit. The "you must meet" party was a sitter, but could scarcely be repeated. We were even reduced to suggesting to Willie that for a theatre, he would like to "see something French by the French Comedy people." Long damped down in the fungoid undergrowth of Hollyhock Lodge, the libidinous spark in Willie's eye did flutter precariously to life for a moment: and

[1] On the way back Willie tried to steer Edward past the Fullers' cottage because Rene, the little girl, usually said "Good morning, sir," to Willie. But instead of Rene it was Jeff who sarcastically said "'Ullo" and winked sadistically at Edward, looking straight past Willie. It was the only bit of luck Edward had that day.

Edward enjoyed watching it slowly fade through five acts of Racine and the Comédie Française. Any suggestion by Willie that he wanted to be taken somewhere "off the beaten track" received a response of enthusiastic agreement from us. We took him to the little Latvian restaurant on the third floor of the tenement behind the Middlesex Hospital, which Willie well believed to be Soho because we drove through Soho to get to it. Here meals were served, swimming in oil, in the kitchen itself: and it was here, we felt, that we were really repaying Willie for those Hollyhock Lodge Sunday evening snack-and-wet-tomato feasts.

Willie countered rather finely by "finding the whole thing tremendously entertaining", and by bringing his dog, a clumber spaniel, who was not only indescribably unsuitable for London but had an almost visible odour of her own which quietly outshone the rancours of Latvian oil. Edward's riposte was neat one.

"That dog needs exercise," he said.

"Yes," said Willie. "But where are you going to get it, in the Brickyard?" This was Willie's name for W.1.

"Take it for a run on those lovely little stretches of grass alongside Mount Street," said Edward. "Tell the man in charge you're a friend of mine."

He was referring of course to Cutts, the most feared Park Keeper in Southern England, who always stood motionless in the centre of these tiny public gardens, his cheek twitching. As is well known he allows no dog to pass him unless it has a muzzle and a lead of tested steel shackle. If the dog pauses in some trance or even slows down he will at once shout "Keep that animal out of it," running the words together in one rasp.

Generalised Off-puts

G. Odoreida, who cannot be described as specifically town or specifically country[1], has developed one or two putting-off ploys equally useful in opposition to either. There is his piano-playing sequence, when he sits down and lets his fingers wander idly over the piano, according to a musical sequence (see later). If Supertown and Supercountry have one weakness in common it is that they become bewildered or uneasy if some average-looking guest starts playing an old piano which has only hitherto been used for some forlorn hope music lessons, which came to an end when she was nine, of the plainest of four daughters.

Then again, Odoreida used to bring with him, in the country on walks, a disguised receptacle of the kind which we call a lifeprop. In it was a collection of deaf aids. No need to thrash out here the old question of whether there was really anything wrong with Odoreida's hearing. The fact is that he sometimes scored points in both camps with these aids. Supercountry might take him for Willie's muddy country walk through woods. O. would carry what seemed to be a large binocular case over his shoulder.

[1] In the country he gives the impression of being more naturally at home in London, and *vice versa*.

W. WESTOVER (*left*) SECRETLY PRIDES HIMSELF ON LOOKING LIKE HIS GAME-KEEPER (*right*). But in practice the result is *vice versa*.

This itself is good, because why does he bring it? Bird watching? But candidly this is never perfectly O.K. with Super-country, because it suggests a slight reproof to the old huntsman, also a very faintly left-wing interest in Nat. Hist., and a suggestion that Supercountry, to whom all birds are some kind of target which he prides himself on being able to distinguish, without raising his eyes, by the sound of the wings, does not know his own job. Pressing the ornithological approach, Odoreida waits for the sound of some woodland bird. At the first "pipple-pipple", he will slowly take out of his case not binoculars, but a small deaf-aid and a packet of sandwiches, will sit down on the newspaper the sandwiches are wrapped in. "Sometimes we have to wait for hours." If Supercountry says "What for?" Odoreida has a special way of saying "Sh". Willie waits in agony, afraid of looking a fool in the eyes of Jack Minton, of point-to-point fame, who often walks this way.[1]

[1] In London circles Odoreida would go in for small tremendously up-to-date deaf aids, suggesting for instance that his cuff button was a disguised microphone, and hold this practically against the lip of

A Note on the Piano-playing of Odoreida

How to be good at the piano without being able to play much really. Here is a theme which has been so much part of my own life in music that I scarcely regard it, any longer, as a problem. It is an approach to musicianship which many senior students of Gameslife besides Odoreida have picked up, I suppose, from my own method. Yet the approach remains empirical. The technique has never been properly cleaned up by Yeovil Arts. The Post Free fifteen and sixpenny pamphlet, *You, Too. In Three Lessons*, was never published, owing to the War; but my thoughts often returned to it, during the immediate post-war years.

Maybe this is a task for Canada. Meanwhile, to set the ball rolling, let me jot a hint, indicate a line of appropriate elaboration.

"Piano Tutors", and teachers in general, make the mistake of telling beginners how to play some rather feeble song or tune, some simple version of "Tea for Two" or "The Ash Grove" or even "God Bless the Prince of Wales". *What is the use of this?* How totally out of key it is with any conceivable lifesituation.

the speaker who is trying to tell the funny story which depends for its effect entirely on intonation.

Against somebody who starts off "Look here Odoreida I'm never absolutely clear what it is you *do*. Civil Servant or something?" Odoreida is very good, especially with the big domineering man Adcock, a typically Supertown who says this sort of thing. He takes out a different instrument—actually an ordinary microphone with a wire attached—makes Adcock (who has a fibrosed knee) climb over a small couch crowded with people, and leads him to a dark corner where he plugs his microphone in and then says "Would you mind saying that again more slowly—and rather more quietly please."

TRY TO SUGGEST THAT YOUR PIANO IS IN CONSTANT USE.

No one, I said to myself when I started on my pil-grim's progress to pianohood, really wants, that is to say truly and deeply wants, to hear me play The Ash Grove.[1]

What is wanted, if one can only do a tiny scrap, is the suggestion when doing the tiny scrap that one could do much more, if one was playing on the sort of piano which appeals to one but one can't, and to the kind of people one likes, which one isn't.

No need to detail the sixty different ways of making sure, if there is a piano in the room, that somebody will say, "Do you play?"

"No" is *wrong* answer to this question. *Right* is "Yes—far too much I'm afraid. But never in public. The point is that I learn music that way. It's the only way I can learn—by letting it soak in through

[1] Nor even the Chopin Prelude which is short and quick and slow and potty and keeps repeating the phrase Ma *Ma* Ma-ma Ma Ma.

56

the fingers." The expert pianoman, holding out his fingers flabbily as if they were made of blotting-paper, can then show that he is pretty adept in almost every known branch of music.

First of all, while still standing, play three quick chords, very firm and staccato, like a piano tuner.[1] Then while sitting down do a short trill on the note B (month's practice). Then go from this trill into the first ten chords of the Siegfried Idyll. Why the Siegfried Idyll? First, because, although to those who happen to know it, 1 in a 1000, it is by no means particularly O.K., to the rest it sounds mysterious and poetical: second, because it is possible by playing this an octave higher or lower, and then again by playing it with the left hand coming down after the right, to suggest that you are extemporising variations on this theme.

Next, to show that you can't simply just play chords but must have technique as well, you must play something with a run in it. This is always the difficulty, but if you really can only just play one scale with the right hand, the scale of C, do it and say, "Do you remember that lyrical Juliet theme in the Prokoviev—and Ulanova seeming scarcely to touch the ground?"

For modern music, I play any small tune, with simple harmony, but the bass note always the same. Try this with Au Clair de la Lune. Finally, when audience begin to look stuffy and depressed it is

[1] Some knowledge of the notes up to late kindergarten standard is essential. It is not enough to be able to spot middle C just because it is opposite the key-lock which fastens the lid.

essential to suggest that you can do jazz as well. I used to play, and keep on playing, the basic bass of boogiewoogie with the left hand, then twice rhythmically but bangingly bring down the flat of my right hand on some patch in the treble.

III

LIT

Recent Work in Litero Creato-Critical Fields

1. How Stands Reviewmanship Today?

IT IS SAID, and we hope it is true, that it is in
creation more than criticism that our ambitions lie.
But Reviewmanship is an old Lifestudy, constantly
being improved and re-codified. A few recent de-
velopments may be worth recording.

The actual definition of reviewmanship is now, I
think, stabilised. In its shortest form it is "How to
Be One Up on the Author Without Actually Tam-
pering With the Text". In other words, how, as
critic, to show that it is really you yourself who
should have written the book, if you had had the
time, and since you hadn't, you are glad that someone has, although obviously it might have been
done better.

New Wording for the Special Subject Review

Suppose the book is on a specialist's subject like
Rhododendron Hunting in the Andes. No known
reviewerman will have been to the Andes; few will
understand the meaning of the word "Rhododen-

I was amazed by the sheer power . . .

I was staggered that so eminent a scholar as Dr. Whitefeet . . .

I was moved by this simple tale of young love . . .

dron". But only the novice will take refuge in vague praise, will speak of the "real contribution to our knowledge of the peaks in the Opeepopee district" or the "debt we owe to Dr. Preissberger, the author". Much better to take the "yes-but" approach, look up in any botanical manual the Latin name of any Rhododendron not listed in Preissberger's index, and say, "Dr. Preissberger leaves the problem of *Azalea phipps-rowbothamii* entirely unanswered". Or start, "It is surprising that so eminent a scholar as Dr. Preissberger . . ." and then let him have it.

New Novels

That is the rough pattern for reviewing any specialist's book. Reviewing novels is a more difficult problem and may even entail actual reading of the first and last chapters. If you don't know what it's all about by Page 12, it is perfectly fair to say that the book is "slow getting started" and

60

that the "plot is involved". Always quote something from the middle pages to show that you've thoroughly studied the book.

A sound general gambit, if there is a love interest, is to single out words and phrases like "sensual", "full lips" or "soft arms," string these together with little dots in between, and then go into a tremendously open-air early morning mood, pervade your article with the atmosphere of putting a big pipe in your mouth and say you are longing for a breath of fresh air. "Thank goodness this is not typical of our younger generation," you say, as if spraying disinfectant, and talk, in general, as if ordinary physical love was only gone in for by irregularly developed persons living in basements. But remember, when reviewing novels, that you are always ready to give a helping hand to the young. The general rule here is to praise, even overpraise,

What a pity . . . **we** miss the true *saeva indignatio* . . .

. . . it leaves an exceptionally nasty taste in the mouth

. . . I found myself unable to put the book down.

any first novel, reserving to yourself the right, which you will invariably exercise, to pitch into No. 2 ("which shows little of the promise of . . .")

Hamlet is a Lousy Farce

In other words, place one mood in the irrelevant context of a totally disconnected one. This ploy goes for both fiction and non-fiction. Say, for instance, of a treatise on infant mortality in nineteenth-century debtors' prisons, that you "are afraid the author takes himself very seriously". But if the subject is the Game of Badminton or the History of the Light Programme, do not fail to regret the jocular tone, nor to be surprised that, in this context, the author should be so anxious to indulge his facility for humour.

Jeffrey was a rotter, but . . .

Certainly the reviewer must remember his status as a Friend of Literature, so let him be careful not to pitch into poets, particularly good ones. When he does, he must show not only that he regrets it, but that he could have eliminated a few of the more important of the author's errors if only he had taken the obvious course of confiding in the reviewer before publication and shown him the manuscript. We can't all be Yeatses. For criticism, it is quite a good thing to take any three consecutive words at random, and say you have studied this passage and that, and that when you were first led into the mysteries of language, you were taught that words have meaning. Then, warmheatedly, talk of Yeats as if he was a sort of simplified Macaulay, and that every word he wrote was clear to the merest schoolboy, and none the worse for that.

When discussing translations of poetry, the Critic is on surer ground. If (1) the poetry is translated from French or German, it is easy to suggest that as everybody is completely at home with French and German anyhow, why translate it at all? If, on the other hand, (2) the original language is rather less well known, Hungarian or Syriac, it is still possible to say: "In the second stanza Mr. Snyder is in deep waters. In his version the 'brown flurry of wings' hastens 'the thickening twilight'. Let us turn to the original for a moment. How much more beautiful and, of course, more Syriac in spirit, is . . ." Translations from the Chinese (3) are inclined to be rather successful and difficult to criticise. S. Spender well says that it is always possible to suggest that "one needs the Chinese calligraphy for full appreciation".

2. The Manship of Memoirs

"Anybody can criticise"—how often have I said this, not for students, to whom I rarely speak, but to Staff. "But how few do." "I mean *do*," I said, walking up and down the Common Room, while they sat wondering. "Do, DO."

They looked at me queerly. We had just been working on this critical section. "We too should not be afraid of criticism."

"Do what?" asked Cogg stickily. Cogg kept a diary

which a publisher had once asked to see, and felt several points up so far as "do" was concerned.

"Yes, what?" said Sticking, who did oil paintings on wooden boards, absolutely untaught, in his bedroom.

"We should write ourselves," I said. "Stick our necks out."

"What!" said Gattling, heartily.

"Of course we could always write our autobiographies," said Cannery. "That would be dead right for 1958."

I wanted the suggestion to come from them. After all G. Wert and Effie Scudamore had written their autobiographies, and so had Sticking Minor, as we called Sticking's nephew, and he had had his published, perhaps because he was only seventeen.

I did not make it an order but soon pencils were out, and I had them all sitting round the Common-room table, making a start.

Before long Autobiography Hour was an institution on alternate evenings. I sat in a corner stimulating the laggards; but on the whole they went to it with a will. The Lawrenceman was the most difficult. "My life—what *is* my life," he was always saying; and he strode to the window to stare at the low sun over the corner of the gasometer. "To write it in a room—behind glass?" he said. "Perhaps, when saxifrage grows on the walls, and the roof is open to sky and stars—perhaps then." But the greatest difficulty was Gattling-Fenn, who rather surprisingly sat hunched up over his blank paper and

AUTOBIOGRAPHY HOUR.

Left to right: Lawrenceman, Cannery (taking mint ball from desk),
Odoreida, Sticking, Cogg-Willoughby, Gattling-Fenn. Although we
did not know it at the time, Odoreida is simply copying long bits
from the *Journals* of André Gide.

could think of nothing to say, not even with the help
of an occasional gin and tonic.

The strange thing was that Gattling started better
than any of us. His idea was to begin with a sort of
it-was-fun-while-the-going-was-good book.

I applauded this until I read the following passage. I don't think people who know us well would
say that Gattling had travelled more than myself.
In fact we neither have. With this in mind, let us
examine the following passages from his first
chapter:

> Over the desert the African wind plays queer tricks,
> and our tiny single-engined Kalaad, flying much too
> low I thought, began to buck and slide alarmingly

in the surface eddies. Passengers were on the verge of panic and it was a nice decision whether to go forward to try and cajole our dark-skinned pilot (of the voluble gestures) to climb the obvious 6,000 feet, or to sit back and try to look bored as if everything was alright. I decided on the latter course. If "Engleesh thinks O.K." then, by some mysterious Law of the Tribes, everybody can feel safe.

Now I took the trouble to check back on this page because this was the first I'd ever heard of G. flying dangerously anywhere. He would have mentioned this about a million times if he'd ever done it. Of course we all knew that he had once taken this sea voyage to Gibraltar—the longest of his life—and had stayed there for a week at the small Stratford Hotel run by this Mrs. Fenwick. What I did not realise was that on the Tuesday of this week he had taken one of the little Taylor Bros air-buses on the day-trip to Algiers and that this did involve, if you counted the very dried up little playground behind the Algiers-Astor where they had failed to make the golf course, flying over something which might be called a desert.

I took G. to task for this, and I am sorry now that I did so; because from that moment his inspiration faded and he never really got back his confidence. There were times when the spark returned, and he said that the only question was whether his was going to be the sort of life which would be serialised by the *Sunday Times* or the *Sunday Express*. He thought he could make great use of 1940, and the fact that at that time the Home Guard at Hale (a place just outside Manchester where he had been platoon commander) had been asked to man, in their exercises, a line from Hale Golf Course starting at the old eighteenth tee and ending at the branching of A56. He said that he expressed an opinion, in a mock exercise against Moodhams Enamel Company Home Guard (Moodhams Enamel Company being supposed to be the enemy), that the line should extend as far as The Grapes, Moberley. Well whether they had agreed with him or not, and this he couldn't remember, Gattling became possessed with the phrase "I Disagree with High Command", and kept repeating it to himself: whereas we thought that even to suggest such a chapter-heading might put the *Sunday Times's* back up, and no good could come of that. If he could have a hint of physical danger in his life, we said to Gattling, who was a shade too young for War No. 1, and hopelessly too old for No. 2, it would be better. But he hadn't. In the end we invented "three years of his life, 1938–41, of which he could neither speak nor write," and he "must crave the reader's pardon for this gap in my brief story". This idea was the best thing that happened to Gattling-Fenn, because it bridged over the time when he was being public relations officer in a firm which specialised in disinfectants—an unsuccessful episode in Gattling's career.

Another suggestion we had for Gattling, talking it over among ourselves, was that he should make use of the very fact of this bad luck of nothing ever happening. Coad-Sanderson had read some Life of some quite good essayist who was also in the Home Office. There was a splendidly long passage in this autobiography taken up in a completely O.K. way by a youthful experience which for some reason "meant" something to this man. It was about standing by some lock and watching the lock gates being worked, so that the flooding in of the water, and the punts and an old barge floating up underneath him started a new chapter in his life, and that the old floating bits of straw and one empty packet of ten Players "shone with hidden gold". Everybody agreed that this section was so good that Gattling could use something, pretty well anything, like this and that it ought to fill up about eight pages. The great question was what. We all chewed this over. "The first thing I remember was being frightened of the knife-cleaning machine: it made me cry, and the smell of knife-powder made me sick," Gattling said. That was

good, but we all believed Gattling could do something better. The youthful visual experience which we chose in the end for Gattling was the soda-water syphon on the small sideboard in the corner of the Fenns' living room which Gattling's father used to visit about ten times an evening. We explained to Gattling how to say that he suddenly really saw what it looked like.

"I should think I did really see it," said G.

"No, we mean see," we said, making a

very slight pause before the word "see", and slightly narrowing our eyes—all very annoying to Gattling, but we were of course helping him, and we took over for him, describing the spot of light gleaming and sliding on the spout of the syphon, as the bottle was tipped and retracted, tipped and retracted, and the impulsive plunge of the soda into the glass, making a gimlet-hole in the shallow pond of honey-coloured whisky.

"Shallow?" said Gattling, boringly still not seeing the point. "To my recollection the whisky was at least the equivalent of a pub treble."

This ran to six pages but we were still badly short of things to say. By the time we had got Gattling to his thirty-fifth year we were only on p. 19—ridiculous. Really up against it, I exercised my right of issuing a circular letter to Lifemen overseas, explaining our difficulty and asking for suggestions. Samarkand (Idaho) wrote back at once. "The usual thing in our autobiogs," they said, "is to have the hero get repeated to him some wise old remark made by some tremendous old character: but the remark must be really thunderously obvious—so much so that even hero understands it. The ideal is for the thing to have the words 'root' or 'soil'." Thank you, Samarkand, but it's space-filling, not half a page, that we want. Very much better was the suggestion from Florida that though outwardly things were pretty smooth with Gattling, he was in fact slowly dwindling away from some obscure complaint, and that nobody was to know what this was, not even Gattling, though in retrospect it becomes obvious in a hundred ways. The Florida people had made a small study of this important gambit, and though they were not able to help much with our immediate problem, it became a stock subject, last Christmas, for discussion groups (Christmas 1957). Memoirmanship apart, to what extent is it possible to concentrate attention on oneself by looking poorly? To what extent does it depend on the profile? Look carefully at the drawing opposite, part of a local collection made by the Florida branch of Gameslife Research American. Study the deflection of the delicate head of the reclining girl. How she assumes a wan cheerfulness, to avoid giving sufferings to others. Even the game of croquet is stopped, so that the visitors can gather solicitously round. Lopsy MacGregor, the little black boy, is miserable. Even the dog feels that there is something wrong with his beloved mistress.

Yet in fact the picture is a perfect illustration of our theme, provisionally described as the inverse equilibrium of the slight headache and the well-shaped nose. True, the name of this reclining person is Dora de la Foissette Gastervil, but study the picture again, more carefully. The croquet players, the solicitous guests, are the victims. Genuinely worried, they are dupes. But the coloured boy obviously knows something. The relations, in the distance, have their back to the scene. Is the dog concerned, or merely recognising a familiar odour? Why has the garden gone to ruin, the chickens running wild? T.B.? No. Dora is suffering from the

most appalling hangover, and is still on an eight-day jag. The cooling drink Lopsy has been bribed to bring her is nine-tenths rye—Old Grandma, double proof. And the time is ten o'clock on a Sunday morning.

In other words, the guests are deceived because the profile is more significant than the complaint. So far as Gattling is concerned, of course, the only thing wrong with him is that he suffers from eczema between the shoulder-blades in spring. But whatever was wrong with him, Gattling's vaguely rugger look would stop this suffering episode from being, autobiographically, of any use to him.[1]

[1] To decide which members of staff or students reached "mean inverse profile requirement" of invalid ploy we had life-size repro-

The curious thing about Cogg-Willoughby was that so far as his autobiography was concerned his difficulty was almost exactly the same as Gattling-Fenn's—very little happened to him. To begin with he was far more diffident about this than Gattling. He did make some notes under the heading of "Chapters out of Childhood"—an excellent title we all thought, and a good theme; because although his childhood was unusually uneventful, it was a Micky Spillane thriller compared to his early man-hood and middle age, when the most important thing that happened to him was the death, in Canada, of a half-sister whom he had not seen since he was six. Everybody agreed that if Cogg's autobiography was worth doing at all, it must depend entirely on the quality of the writing, and indeed Cogg was so con-scious of this fact that he took nearly a fortnight writing the first two hundred words, although we were all around, on tap to help him with this business of the quality of the writing. One of Cogg's difficulties was that he had an extremely bad memory. "An absolute must is your prep school," we said. There are only two things he could think of: one was that he was once top of his form for parsing, and the other was a boy whose nickname was "Uncle" to whom during the autumn term Cogg

duction of this drawing pasted on three-ply, with a hole cut out in place of Dora's face through which volunteer could place head. Rather an interesting example this of our care for detail. It is also of interest, showing the difficulties of the total ploy, that no member of the staff when tested produced a positive result. This is an instructive experiment for the week-end shooting party or Boys' Club, and will break the ice indeed at any sticky gathering.

used to give an expensive firework once a week to bribe him out of throwing Cogg into a furze bush. There was an obvious chance here of building up Cogg as a man whose whole character was warped by being bullied; although there is a smaller group which remembers Cogg's rather horrid treatment of Mather, at Tidworth O.T.C. camp. It is they who say that it was Cogg who was the bully, and that this is the fact which tainted his later life and left the trauma.

Later we went over this ability of Cogg's to win a prize: but it was not so fruitful as it at first seemed. "You never had any difficulty with languages of course," we suggested; and an interesting point came up here. Because Cogg's mother was half French, it was always regarded as absolute gospel that Cogg was bi-lingual. Actually this was far from the case, though he did evolve a series of valuable ploys to support this idea. If ever French had to be spoken he would always shut up dead or start reading a book, somehow suggesting that the sort of French we were using would fall to pieces instantly if he introduced the real thing. Occasionally people would ask him questions about French, and he managed these extraordinarily well. "Now Cogg, what's the French for a 'boarding house'?"

Cogg would not look up. "There is really no word, interestingly enough."

I wasn't going to let him get away with this so I said, "But what about *pension*". Cogg looked expressionless for a second; then he said:

73

"That is the vocabulary-book word, but—danger. *Pension* suggests a whole tribe of associations which simply do not exist in England." As Cogg's vocabulary was only about fifty words he did well I think at this point by saying, "Actually one should use a phrase. If you wanted to be colloquial you could say *coup de maison*".[1]

Fowlering Up

Sometimes I am quite proud of my little band of "Merry Memoirists," as I call them—we have plenty of chaff during break. But when we were in the midst of our difficulties with Gattling, I could not help noticing the change in Cogg-Willoughby, who to start with had been a good deal slower even than Gattling. When we were all sitting round at the autobiography-writing-table, scratching our heads, it began to be annoying to see Cogg scribbling away without a moment's pause. Now this is a fine ploy in the examination room. I have used it myself. Nervous candidates, unable to make a single movement of their pen, sit watching you, transfixed.

Cogg was annoying us. It became essential to

---

[1] Cogg made endless use of this *coup de*. There was another thing he thought he knew about French, and he built a tremendous lot of his language life round it. And that was that the accent in French words "always comes on the last syllable". He would bring in half-Anglicized proper names like Avignon and hit the last syllable with an "ong" like *Queen Mary's* hooter. In a restaurant he would always ask, as his first thing, for Pâté Maison, partly because he had learnt how to accent these syllables like the opening phrase of the Fifth Symphony.

"stop flow", as we used to say in the crude but happy days of early Gamesmanship. It is essential in a corporate community to discourage the disagreeably outstanding. As I explained to my good friends, *we were a team* of autobiog. writers. With my more or less commissioned *Literary Guide to the Thames Valley* on the stocks I felt justified in checking Cogg myself; and I did it by a very simple method which I have used for about thirty years and which I call Fowlering Up. You look over the shoulder of the writer and make a yes-but comment on something minutely verbal. Start smoothly by saying, "I shall like this, I know. Yes, you're using the word 'cathedral' in the right sense, I think." That was the word Cogg was writing. He seemed to take no notice.

Later I said "Yes . . . 'the monks intone' . . ." Then I twirled round quickly with my face practically touching Cogg's and said "Why not say 'chant'?"

"Why should I?" said Cogg.

"Shorter—simpler."

"It's only a letter shorter," said Cogg.

"More English?" I said. But you can never trust Cogg. Feeling that he was going to prove the word was Dutch or something, I tried to be more general, and quickly. I read again, over his shoulder.

" 'The lights came on one by one'—isn't that rather a coincidence?" I was trying to appear to be appearing to try not to be patronising. Cogg did slow down a little, when I said this.

"I mean aren't you a tiny bit bemused by the

phraseology of your own pet phrases . . . a little bit
pen-proud . . . what you-know-who would call
a Grace?" Sure enough Cogg's pen did begin to
drag a little bit—a little bit as if he was writing in
treacle.

I had expected Sticking to have little difficulty
with his own memoirs: but although he speaks so
readily in his clear way and has more wit in his talk
than most of us, as soon as he started to write the
blood seemed to ebb from the expressive centres of
his brain and all that was left by the falling tide was
a lot of verbal old iron. Words like "federation",
"workers", "natural evolutionary processes", "pro-
duce" and even "proletariat" kept turning up. "You
must be more personal," I said, looking over his
shoulder. "Detail. For Heaven's sake look at this:
"My part in the development of the Workers' Educational movement in East Anglia . . ."

"Pure heaven," said Cannery.

"What did you actually *do*?" I kept urging. Sticking became uneasy.

By a series of cross-questions it turned out that
Sticking's only concrete memory of this was bi-
cycling along a muddy lane near Hay Tor with one
of his students, a girl with a long fair pigtail.
He had been lecturing on Town Planning to the
Colchester Borough Council Management Summer
School.

In the end, curiously, we found it better to make
Sticking concentrate on his spare-time fondness for

the arts. "Music is my real life", became the start of chapter six. He had a complete collection of Elgar, *The Ring*, and any works by the Big Six of the great Germans which were called on the label, whatever the facts, "posthumous". Sticking always wanted an audience for his music, and because we all liked him we stuck to a secret rota so that there were always two detailed to listen. But as he kept his gramophone in his bedder, and as it was of rather an old-fashioned make and  would only take 78s, which were lying all over everything everywhere, it was difficult to move a step without making a sound like the delicate crunching of sea-shells.

But those who expected bold attacks from Sticking were disappointed. If he wrote things about "the uniform of convention," it would mean that he had seen a lot of people wearing white ties at a performance of *Fidelio* at Covent Garden in 1936. He actually seemed to prefer, when he went to the theatre, going up the back stairs to a converted schoolroom in a district north of Camden Town with an unheard-of postal number. Later in his book he did rather well by describing a radio talk which he had suggested and which was "mysteriously turned down" by the B.B.C.

Odoreida presented a different problem. "Frank-ness is everything in autobiography," I had told my little band. "Right," said Odoreida and began a series of recollections almost all of which, in spite of what I had said, simply had to be cut out. For instance few people know that he was nearly two terms at Oxford University before he was asked to leave. How did Odoreida get to Oxford? As a 1923 equivalent of a Displaced Person? Displaced from what? Did he himself invent the name of the "University of the Jamaican Dutch" which he represented as part of the special student exchange Peace Across the Waters agreement, something which "embodied surely one of the best of the Liberal movements floated after Oners*"? Or did Odoreida invent this phrase himself? Was Professor Gilbert Murray, who "was so gracious to me", really Odoreida's dupe? And even if not, does this make good auto-biographical reading? Anyhow most of us agreed that he couldn't possibly say he was sent down for the thing he was sent down for, because however frank the self-revelation, no one could ever possibly put that particular thing in a book, discreditable as it was in a way so uniquely combining the unpleasant and the uninteresting. After a lot of discussion it was decided to suggest that the disciplining should fol-low some incident, which though true was less derogatorily vapid. In the end, pointless as even this was, we advised Odoreida to record those days

*Odoreida likes making little jokes, but these are always about totally unfunny subjects—e.g. calling World War I and II "Oners" and "Twoers".

in Eights Week when he used to wear an Oxford "Blue" tie, though he was never a Blue nor the least fraction of one. This act was so astounding to some that they could not bring themselves to look squarely at the woolly dark-blue tie and scarf Odoreida put on. When he was challenged Odoreida would not defend himself. He would say that he had always wanted to be able to wear the tie or ties: so as he was not given it, he bought one. We decided Odoreida should put this in his chapter on Oxford—"I Wake up the Spires". "No doubt the authorities," it ran, "no doubt the powers that be found it difficult to stomach this affront to tradition and 'correct' behaviour. They cut me out of their friendly activities, particularly their boating dinners. My attitude hardened. Had one of them come forward with one genuinely friendly gesture, one handshake which was really warm . . ."

In the end we had to veto so many of Odoreida's suggestions, including three complete chapters, that he became huffy and said he'd scrap the whole thing, which he did. Instead he wrote a long autobiographical novel, solely in order to introduce a character whom he called Querula Minge, quite obviously meant to be Eva Plimm, so that he could go for this girl as hard as he could and simply tear her to pieces. All this was because she had told Odoreida, when he tried to kiss her during some long train ride they had to take together down to H.Q., that his ears smelt like tarpaulin.

3. TO WHAT EXTENT IS THERE A VIRTUAL SUPERLECTURE?

The other day I was thumbing through one of the early volumes of my 600-page folio notebooks,[1] repository of all the first sketches and miscellaneous thoughts of Lifemanship, quarries out of which, from such obscure jottings as "how about antisepsis" ... "REN 6382" ... "6 South African Sherry" are built what are to become the completed chapter. I found an entry with Lecturemanship written beside it in blue pencil. I had obviously given some lecture where there had been a few empty back rows. I began scribbling notes. Here is the result.

Chairman Play

Let me give a little shape to these jottings. One of the best ways of being one up in a lecture is not to lecture but be chairman. Chairmaning—the art of being one up on the lecturer—has been independently well described by J. Priestley.[2] It is the art by which the Chairman can *break flow* of lecturer with such basic and even dramatic ploys as having little notes passed up to him and then making

---

[1] Natually a large proportion of the pages are blank, and will be kept so, I hope, in the eventual printing by the Facsimile Society, since surely this very blankness is indicative of a significant mood, of a pause in process, a change of direction even, though the order and the placing of the blank pages may be sometimes in doubt.

[2] *Delight.*

tiny "unobserved" signals to people in the audience.[1]

Simpler methods do not need less practice. The Chairman who remains on the platform for the lecture should certainly have something distracting about him—he may cross his right leg over his left and reveal the fact that right sock is so shrunk that it scarcely comes above the shoe at all. Audience will watch this large white naked ankle. If his hands are rather red and puffy naturally, he may let one hand hang by his side with an inert look as if he had some deformity, slight, and possibly recent, but certainly growing worse. Occasionally I have seen a Chairman do well by coming on to the platform with three large books of his own, one obviously actually written by him (name big on dust jacket), and keeping these under his arm during the lecture as if he was just popping in, between two really important lecture engagements of his own, in order to give a hand to old Layman. He can establish this point in his opening speech by making two jokes of intensely local reference, about some unpopular fire drill, which he knows his audience will laugh at, though the point will be completely incomprehensible to the visiting lecturer, who will look uneasy.

Longer practice is required for what I call the off-beat laugh. This is really a slow chuckle developed during some serious part of the lecture as if Chair-

[1] Odoreida, when Chairman, was able to suggest that the note contained rather bad news of a derogatory personal nature.

man was trying to lead the audience into the realisation that there really was, after all, some grain of amusement in what Lecturer was saying. While thus smiling or giving a relishing chuckle, Chairman may turn, not his head, but his whole torso, in the direction of the clock, suggesting that he wants to know how the time is going in as unobvious a way as possible. Another way to do this is to take a quick glance at the wrist-watch, but to have this strapped so high up that forearm that it takes a lot of covert arm-extension to get there.

At the end of the lecture the Chairman can get up after a short pause, with a start, so as to suggest "Why has he suddenly left off talking?" He may then say, "Well, I am sure there will be lots and lots of you'll be wanting to ask questions and I am very glad Dr. Layman has agreed to do this. Now then . . ." It is perfectly easy by the intonation to discourage the asking of any questions whatever.

After no pause at all Chairman can then say, "Well, if you won't I will. I am going to sail right into it. Now Doctor, what exact evidence have you of your interesting suggestion about the I.Q. of Scottish children being higher north of Glasgow?"

Needless to say Dr. Layman will stammer, if only because he never mentioned I.Q.s at all; while the impression remains that Chairman has gone rather more deeply into the subject than the lecturer.

Gattling-Fenn

Gattling always interested me on the platform. He once studied a book called *How to Think Fluently On Your Feet*. One rule was "Be economic of gesture". Taking an occasional glance at his feet Gattling used to stand to attention through his whole lecture until he came to a bit where he said "the whole edifice of modern civilisation is beginning to sway, before it crashes to the ground in flames." When he got to "sway" he would use one of the gestures illustrated by a diagram in the book but not in my view the right one—a quick zig-zag movement of the right hand ending in a loop "to suggest some phase of the argument was finished"—and *invariably* he barked his knuckles on the rostrum. Our audience of young people warmly applauded but I am not certain that he had really what we call "got" his audience.

Later, Gattling changed styles to a kind of higher chatmanship, or speaking easily without notes, which was a bad choice because unless he had everything written out in full, he could never think of anything to say after about four minutes, and so had to use a lot of ploys to fill up time. One of these was to read out of a book. Realising quite rightly that it is a bad thing to come in with a book stuffed full of paper-markers like feathers, and that this suggested careful preparation which is unsuitable for chat specialists, he would pretend to find the passage in his book by rifflng through the pages, really getting almost at once because of a piece of chewing gum he stuck in the page he wanted—typical Gattlingism, because more often than not he had to tear the pages apart with both hands. But I must say he had a wonderful way of closing the book after reading. I remember him once, badly stuck, opening at random a book left over from the last lecture, something about the History of Chartered Accountancy. After he'd finished it he looked deeply at the audience, while at the same time closing the book very slowly, almost with a faint suggestion, as it were, that it was practically the Bible, a ploy which once nipped in the bud a slow handclap.[1]

In later life Gattling only gave one lecture—on the contrast between English and American humour—whatever the announced subject. He would pull out his dog-eared notebook and begin: "Today, if I am interpreting your Chairman's wishes correctly, in speaking about the 'Gothic in Art', I will approach it specially from the standpoint of the contrast between English and American humour."

The danger here, of course, is that by some curious law, if you do this, you will see sitting in the middle of the front row somebody who listened to your lecture last week on Ralph Waldo Emerson,

[1] For after-dinner speeches Gattling would write hundreds of words of notes on the back of old menus which he used to collect for this purpose, pretending, on the night, that this was the menu for this dinner, to suggest that if he was using notes, they were scribbled during the speech of the previous speaker. His next-door neighbours were always getting hold of Gattling's old menu by mistake, and it was amusing to see a man who thought he was going to get lobster *thermidor* being served with pressed duck.

and who is going to be tremendously surprised to find that your Gothic in Art piece is precisely the same. This calls for bold gamesplay. You must say that you are "delighted to see somebody in the audience who can confirm the difficulty we had in defining these principles in terms of Emerson," and "wonder if they will approve of this new formula". Say also, if necessary, that this person "asked a very interesting and profound question" which although, of course, untrue, will confuse and at the same time compliment this prospective enemy and the chances are he will string along.[1]

Cogg-Willoughby and the Distinction Ploy

Of all the basic techniques of this art the one I most admire and the most difficult to perform is the Distinction Ploy. I am not in fact referring to the effortless superiority of the man who combines knowledge with understanding, wisdom with learning, and clearness of aim joined to integrity of social

[1] Gattling's attempts at gesture were tremendously developed by our Dramaship Instructor, G. Wert, who was a great sight on the platform. He used hundreds of gestures but they were all somehow like a repertory production of *The Beggars Opera*. We could never understand why he had never been asked to speak on the B.B.C. television, particularly as "How to speak on Television" was one of the courses he most specialised in. I can see him now saying "The atomic bomb can destroy a city the size of Wallingford like puffing out a candle—" (he said Wallingford because, although it isn't a city, that was the place the Chairman came from). Then he would turn full on the Chairman, hold out his closed fist and say, "But it cannot make a flower grow". As he said this he opened his fist one finger at a time, about a foot in front of the Chairman's chin, as if it were a flower growing. Privately this amused us because Wert spent hours every winter with an old bag of bulbs, hyacinths, and nothing ever came out of them, except slimy-looking leaves about two feet long.

purpose. One may have a little of that oneself; though even then one sometimes spoils it if, for instance, one misses the first step mounting the platform. No—I am referring to the art of creating the illusion of distinction. Actually our Cogg-Willoughby with his hollowed-out, hankering sort of face made a good shot at it especially if he stood under a top light, and increased this effect by the usual methods of thirty seconds' silence before starting, gazing at his manuscript and slightly shifting it around, with about two very slight coughs. He would sometimes get people really quiet, by taking one small tablet out of a green glass bottle from which a very long tail of cotton-wool had to be pulled before the tablet would come out, and then be stuffed back after. He was able to suggest by this that his stomach was only held in place by one frayed piece of catgut, that he was plucky to be there at all, and that it was only the inly burning fire of the spirit that gave him the strength to raise the chalk to the blackboard.

Mind you, some outside help is of great value to this whole Distinction gambit, and the Chairman must somehow be persuaded, or bribed with a Rover ticket for a Test Match, to inform the audience beforehand, if you are lecturing, say, on Blenheim, (a theme which unless you are careful will need a good deal of mugging up) that you are not only a scholar of the Marlborough campaigns, but that you are so morbidly distinguished that not much information can be expected on such a well-known thing as the Battle of Blenheim from a lecturer who is such a tremendous scholar of his subject that he has spent the last two years studying the commissariat chits, 1704, of the 48th Worcester Horse, a regiment once reviewed by the Duke of Marlborough before the Battle of Oudenarde.

Counter-Inspector Play

No one boasting the name of Lectureman can leave out Tutorial Classmanship and Extension Lecture Play, if only because it is here that we find, essentially, the fine gambitfield surrounding that passionate madcap of the Extension Lecture room, the Inspector. This great bird is by no means universal. It is fairly safe to say that that very fine lifeman W. Auden, delivering his Oxford lecture on Poetry, will not be casting a dozen worried glances at the door in case the Inspector turns up. All the same, when one is lesser, and younger, Inspectors are pretty well inclined to swarm. Now the basic gambit against Inspectors is to be promising, and for that the "background necessity" is to be (a) relatively much younger than the inspector whatever the facts and (b) gauche. *Never try to be distinguished and gauche at the same time.* Change over from Distinguished as soon as the Inspector comes in. In the old days I nurtured my gaucheness for the good start it gave me against the Inspector. This Inspector used to arrive about every tenth lecture.[1] He would sit surrounded by

[1] But of course no good inspectorman would arrive the day he was expected. In later, more experienced days, I used to ring up Inspectors and say "I think you'll enjoy the discussion tonight". Amazingly, it worked. Tipped-off class would respond brilliantly to rehearsed inspector-lecture.

frost in the foreground, not too pleased with his evening journey in his chilly Austin Seven to my Tutorial Class in East Croydon. After listening, bolt upright, for ten minutes, he would put on his glasses and study the printed syllabus of the course, which I had written nine months before and crammed full of stimulating discussion points which I hoped would catch the eye of Mrs. Hobchild, the Director, but which yet had a solid backbone of knowledgeable continuity for Mr. Coldharbor, the Inspector, to approve of. In practice, of course, I never followed my syllabus, nor looked at it even if I could find it.

It was my personal custom, a good one, to talk about whatever book I happened to have been reading the week-end before the lecture.

Mr. Coldharbor, after listening for eight minutes, then put on his glasses and had a look at my syllabus. He found Week Ten, February 4th, 1938, and began reading it, in order to discover what I was supposed to be talking about. A glance over his shoulder told me that he read "Scandinavian Drama and its Influence on the Twentieth Century Renaissance of our Theatre." What I had in fact been talking about when he came in was, because it happened to be the book I was reading on Sunday, the new Life of Isadora Duncan—the part where she renounces marriage bonds as a priest-ridden concept, antagonistic to the fuller life.

I owe so much to the hard schooling, the cut and thrust, of those early days. Looking back I very much doubt whether, now, I could with three swift and easy transitions show the obvious relationship between the first impact of Ibsen's *The Pretenders* and Isadora Duncan's renunciation of her second husband.

Prop Management

Although I myself wear glasses for reading off hidden notes, I have never fully developed Lens Drill. It is rather a good thing and, of course, common practice, when you have at last started a laugh which is liable to stagger on for a moment or two, to take off your glasses slowly and sadly and rub fingers into the tired marks under your eyes. Of course the real expert, making a particularly boring or pointless remark, can sometimes succeed in hypnotising the audience into thinking he has said something effective by speeding up, rapidly diminishing the volume of his voice and dashing his spectacles on to the desk, looking at his audience with corkscrew intentness.

One of the shortest of our lecture experts was "Winkie" Green, who lectured under the name of W. L. St.G. Lauterberg Green. He was for some years very successful with a prop-gambit some have found worth trying. When he first came on to the platform all you could see behind the desk, owing to this shortness, was his hair, upright yet twisted, like sticks of barley sugar. Winkie would then make considerable play of his being too short, sending people to fetch something for him to stand on and pretending to be embarrassed by this, gaining sympathy at the start, though in fact his disability was one of his strongest weapons, and he wore shoes without heels.[1] His prop he used about half-way through the lecture. He once told me that it was a small segment cut out of the top of a discarded hat rack. Anyhow from it seemed to sprout a miniature arrangement of chimney-shaped prongs, of different heights. Whether he was lecturing about Persian rugs or bird-migration, Keats or the meaning of the Primary in the Presidential Election, he would always bring out this old bit of hat rack in the fortieth minute, place it, delicately and precisely, on the table in front of him, take out a very long pencil from the other pocket, and point to some bit of this thing about half-way up one of the chimneys. The audience grew as still as death. "This model gives a very rough idea of relative positions," he would say, stroking the top half of it delicately with the tip of his pencil. "Do

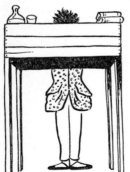

you see that this 'reaction' counterpart is much shorter than is commonly imagined?" There was not a soul in the audience, except, of course, trained Lifemen, who did not feel that this demonstration proved that Winkie was a born lecturer, and that, unlike some, he could give you something to bite on.

[1] Borrowed from an oldish male ballerina.

Counter Chairman

At the beginning of these notes I emphasised the danger, for the lectureman, from his Chairman. Here are a few hints from the best Chairman-squasher I ever knew—Willy Jack:

"In style, be the opposite." If your Chairman is a practised official speaker he probably knows how to tand still and keep his arms folded or relaxed by his sides. Suggest at once that personally you are not that kind of speaker (even if that technique suits the paid agent of some local political club) by allowing your hands to wander aimlessly, sloppily stroking the back of your head or fidgeting with your collar.

Arouse sporting instincts of audience by having slight tremor if you are unfortunate enough to have Chairman who is popular games hero. It may make Chairman hover nervously if you fiddle crossly with the lighting arrangements one minute before starting. If he happens to be enfeebled through age, it may be a good thing to ask him to move a heavy lectern a foot to the right. In general one should be reasonably severe to the Chairman. I have rarely encountered an audience who was not glad to see Chairman snubbed, unless he is an old war-hero or professional ball-game player. Never, on any occasion, make the hackneyed mistake of laughing and shaking your head when Chairman makes his joke or compliment. Always, including and especially when he pays his compliment to you, show no reaction whatever but let your eyes roam coldly yet intently over the faces of your audience, as if you were surprised and interested in something about their physical appearance or nationality. When audience applauds after his introduction of you, clap your own hands twice in a dangling way as if you wanted to make Chairman feel that for once in a while a tiny little bit of the applause was for him.

If Chairman sits on platform it is rather a good thing to turn suddenly full on him, bending your body right towards him, and say, "But I wonder if Dr. Riemann agrees with me?" This will make Dr. Riemann look nervy and mystified and guiltily aware of the fact that he hasn't been attending; and it will suggest to your audience that you wonder privately whether Dr. Riemann is quite the man for his present job.

When the Chairman makes his speech of thanks afterwards still pay no attention. You may smile, but smile half to yourself while busily picking up your papers, packing your glasses, etc., suggesting that for goodness' sake we all of us want to get on with the job, don't we. There are tremendous possibilities in after-the-lecture play. If there is a sort of

TYPICAL ODOREIDAISM

Asked to substitute for speaker at Yeovil Union, and faced by a house three-quarters empty, he steps out and puts up this board.

sandwich-and-coffee period afterwards, mix freely with the young students and talk naturally to them in a light tone. Say very little to the Principal, be coldly courteous to his wife, and say nothing whatever to the man who was your Chairman. Do not even look at him. This will give him the impression, not too brutally I hope, that he has somehow put his foot in it.

4. THE OLD QUOTESMAN

Good Lifemen, returning from abroad, bring back lifeworthy objects for their friends. A dollar forged north of the Arctic Circle, a Highway Patrol identification badge. F. Wilson brought me a sheet of paper with some Chinese printed on it with, as I thought then, the excellent suggestion that I should pin it up in a thin gold frame near the projection on the mantelpiece on which I hang my old rowing cap, and that I should look at it occasionally and say, "Don't you love those lines?" Guest should hesitate. He will probably say:

"What, do you mean you can read that?"

"Give me time—give me time," I reply. "Yes I can read it, I suppose, but don't ask me to translate because I don't think it's translatable."

Then you stare at it and say: "Well, let's have a shot," and you start: "The secret beauty-bird sings —chants—in the magnolia tree—the water buffalo strides in the brown waters of our . . . water margins . . . village pond, I suppose we might say. The

イェイツ「イニスフリイ湖島」

を写し出して、それを讃美するよりも、自分の心の瞬間の望みをここに結晶させたのである。しかしそれだけならば、表現は易しいのである。そして、それのみの表現をしてあれば、その詩は我々に訴える力が薄くなるであろう。イェイツは、この詩の中に、内奥の感情を歌って、人間一般の心に宿っている望みを表わしている。我々はすべて煩わしい現実を離れて、静かな心の安らいを追うという、理想をもつのである。しかもこの詩は、理想を表現するのみではなくして、一種の強い光をきらめかせて、人間の心の中に横わる根本的

scholar sharpens his nails: the sun is setting over the western hills—long shadows creep across the—the City of Exclusion—the Forbidden City, sort of . . . That's very roughly it." The whole thing certainly has a mildly depressing effect on the visitor. But I must mention this incident. The 1000 to 1 chance happened to me, incredibly, the third time I tried this. H. Howse was my guest; and who would guess that such an expert amateur cricketer had taken a First in Oriental languages? "I like your translation," he said; "but isn't that actually a warning against pickpockets?" I turned slowly round. I remembered now what Wilson had told me. He had pulled this thing off the wall of the waiting room of a railway station. If I had been alone with Guest I should have said, "Do you know you're the first person that spotted that?" and tried to create a leg-pull atmosphere. But Withers and Miss Plimm were there, so

I had to try a less familiar counter. "Yes," I said delightedly. "Isn't it a marvellous language? Against pickpockets or 'hand-flickers', isn't it? But of course being Oriental it's all in terms of the 'secret bird', the long shadows and the 'forbidden city' or citadel of private possession." H. Howse made no comment, except to say that if the text was really being reproduced in a book it should be stated that the Chinese was not Chinese at all but a comment, in Japanese, on *The Lake-Isle of Innisfree*.

IV

RECENT WORK

IN ESTABLISHED GAMBITFIELDS

1. New Notes on British Car Play

ONE OF THE BEST-KNOWN chapters of *One-Up-manship* was, I think, miscalled "The Carmanship of Godfrey Plaste". The ploy of Plaste's Placid Salutation spread through the country: but the impetus came much more from the rich gambitfield of *driving* the car, in elaboration of my original definition of carmanship—"How to steal the crown of the road without being an absolute hog". I first formulated it, I remember, when I was alone sitting over the precipice at Cape Wrath, with nothing but kittiwakes and Dr. Longstaff for companions.[1]

Nowadays Plaste and his work are in disrepute. He has spent the last three years fiddling about with impracticable car gambit inventions, the £250 horn (for his £50 car) which can be adjusted by fingertip control to suggest, by its tone, not only such ordinary sounds as the raucous YAH and the lady-like Boo, but more complex ones like "Keep to the left, rescue squad passing" or "Pardon me, madam,

See my *Short List of Places Where it is O.K. for things to come to you first at.*

but if you would do me the privilege of reading the road signs you would realise, I think, that this is my road. All I ask you to do is to keep your car stock still".

Modern car research chooses different fields. Let us ask ourselves "What is the perfect One-Up situation?" Undoubtedly when the car which has just passed you, owing to superior driving or engine power, is copped for speeding while still in view, and, even better, grazes a lamp post as well.

"*Be one thing or the other*"

But this ideal situation is beyond our control. Not so the car itself. This should be either (1) Old or (2) New. Nothing between. The fading three-year-old model, desperately polished up till the chromium begins to wear off, is dubious, unless your ploy is the marvellous something you can't buy now about your wonderful old bus. The very-good-quality gambit, suggesting money without a trace of ostentation, is certainly difficult to counter, although I have one useful recommendation here, I think, which is to say (glancing at friend's black and unobtrusive but fairly powerful 1952 Bentley): "Yes, but cars are basically made of tin anyway, aren't they. Why try and pretend it's eighteenth-century Chipendale?" If your own car is cheap and showy, coloured in alternate panels of ginger and raspberry, you can look at it affectionately and say: "I quite like old Toothpaste Tube here." But in most cases my advice is "Be really new or really old".

If the car is fresh and gleaming, dress the part. Always put on leather gloves (never buttoning them) while driving. Make a tremendous fuss about not leaving day-old newspapers in the back of the car. Let your personality conform. Be inclined, now if never before, to use a masculine but expensive cigarette holder. Clean and empty the ash tray every day. Let it be known that you are of the opinion that "mud unless instantly removed, rots the underside of mudguards". It may even be worth while having your car driven to your house by your garage, for no especial reason. Peter Blond, the racing driver (of Peter Blond Ploys, Inc.) has been a great help to me here. He recommends that if there is a ledge inside below the rear window, let there be put one object only, carefully chosen—perhaps the large long leather of a case of binoculars (unnecessary to buy the binoculars as well). Do not, he says, make the mistake of *gilding*. That is, do not have any accessories whatever (patent fog lamps, offside distance-markers, unusual extra reflectors). "It spoils the line." Practise saying "It spoils the line".

Old Car play is very different in some respects. There is a definite time when new car becomes old car (point of no return to the dealer)—when making a ploy of looking after it changes into making a ploy of not looking after it. A new gash in the wing and you laugh. "It's only hanging by a thread anyway," you say. In fact your whole character alters. Instead of being dependable, husbanding, poised and cleanly, you are now slapdash, open-air, good old Freddie. Change your Christian name if necessary. Be generous in gesture when driving. Leave piles of strongly contrasted objects in the back which yet give a favourable impression of the extraordinary variety of your interests. Squash rac-

FOR NEW MINIATURE CARS: Effect can be heightened by sitting hired chauffeur on two telephone directories.

ket . . . micrometer . . . *Stories of the Great Operas.* Old car should if possible be big. If it is very small as well as old, and unpleasantly refined as well, it may be necessary, on chosen occasions, to have it driven up by a chauffeur, which suggests big new car as well, somewhere in the background.

A sports car is a splendidly one-up possession, and the carman play is to leave it at that. Above all, for instance, do not cover the front with badges and arms of automobile clubs. "There is only one badge which interests me," say. "That little bit of tin which means you've lapped Silverstone at a hundred." If you don't actually have one, use a 98·8 voice here. Then: "They cost about twenty pounds extra, but some think it worth while to buy tyres with RACING stamped on them." Ignorant women and a few men can be impressed by the hot-rod approach, which is basically to let it leak out that the car "isn't quite what it looks". That you've had a Bosch

99

ignition put in, and Frog lighting. Valves ground in Padua. "I had to have this old Vauxhall body to take the 2½ litre."

Of course the skilful passenger can answer back this kind of thing. In the sports car he can say, "I bet she'd really move with the right petrol". Driving smoothly and silently along in his friend's gleaming new solid-worth type model he can say, "I should have that little bbbrrp noise put right at once, tiny as it is."

We most certainly offer people lifts

From time to time new Notes for Driver occur to us. Here are a few.

When you see a friend who obviously wants a lift, offer him a lift. But drive well *past* him before you

CORRECT POSITION FOR SUGGESTING:
"I don't in the least mind stopping to pick you up, but if you *could* get a move on . . ."

stop, shouting in a drill-sergeant voice: "Want a
lift?" This will cause him to take an anxious little run
to catch you up. Ram home this advantage by leaning over him, after he has got in and shut the door,
so as to open the door and shut it again yourself,
suggesting that passenger can't even shut a door,
especially if he has in fact done so.[1] Ask him if he'd
mind moving a little over to the side as he's in the
way of the hand brake, as if the hand brake worked;
speak again about the door, telling him to be careful
not to touch the door handle. Take corners more
swingingly than usual, as you have the steering
wheel to hang on to, he hasn't. If he is smoking,
develop car pride and indicate that he should use
the ash tray. You will point patiently to where it is.
If he uses the electric cigarette lighter—has the
effrontery, that is, to do so without asking—tell him
you'd rather he didn't as it uses up a lot of current.
If he fiddles about with matches, light his cigarette
with lighter yourself, while passing lorry at crest of
bridge. If passenger is made to sit in back seat it is
always possible to make him feel inferior not only
to yourself but to any other passenger in the front
seat, and actually it often works well to put your
own adjustable driving seat back to the full extent
of its runners. As back passenger bends up his
knees, ask him to be careful not to squash the
greengages. Somehow ignore him, as if he were a

[1] The driver is the only effective person by historical right of
assumption. Passenger can not only do nothing; rightly handled he
can know nothing either.

hanger-on. Suddenly bring him into the conversation with some such phrase, half shouted, as: "I'm speaking of Browning *the poet*", suggesting that you are in a half doubt whether he realises that Browning is a poet.

After half an hour stop at a pub suggesting drinks all round in a way which implies that now, surely to goodness, passenger will be relieved to be able to make this slight repayment of your kindness to him. After twenty minutes further driving, do this again.

Of course there are frequent occasions when the carman wants to impress his passenger, especially if she is a woman.[1] R. Cheeseney, the mushroom grower, who fancies himself as one of the "ugly as sin yet a great charmer" boys, prides himself on the ease with which he makes his left-hand gear-change with his right hand while continuing with his left hand to hold the right hand of his lady passenger, or

Cheeseney is now experimenting with holding the right hand of his girl, while driving, with *both* hands while steering *with his knee-caps*, which he presses up against the lower rim of his steering wheel. Some progress has been made.

[1] Godfrey Plaste, naturally cumbersome in a car, and never having possessed one which went more than forty miles an hour, was yet able to impress, some readers may remember, because he had the good idea of practising, for half an hour a day, the difficult trick of reversing. A Worcester girl, Daisy Hopper, is said to have been successfully wooed by Plaste, entirely by this speed in reverse.

even to stroke her knee. Cheeseney is always theorising about car-parking, when taking a girl to the theatre. He has a complicated graph showing exactly how far you can ask what kind of girl to walk from the car to the theatre in what kind of weather when she is wearing what degree of paper-thin-ness of shoe-sole, plus peep-bo big-toe-holes. I have seen this graph, which I am bound to say seems to be designed by Cheeseney to prove the power of Cheeseney over girls in general.

Why I Admired Godfrey Plaste

I admired him, though I never liked him. How many times have I heard it said: "Now he's a good driver." Well of course he is and so are all of us, who have been driving our car for donkeys' years, ten thousand miles per annum plus an occasional trip as far as Avignon or Aberdeen. We never think about it. We do it unconsciously. We are all the same. He is the same. Yet somehow he has made a thing of being a good driver.

He does not do this in the stupid obvious way of dropping hints about earlier experience "on the circuit", though—smart ploy—he often speaks of parts of cars by the French or Italian names for them. I have seen him memorising these, off a chart. Out of a car he is rather a vague man, but inside he suddenly becomes neat. His profile becomes definite and exact. In the car he wears a carefully placed hat. He takes hold of the wheel precisely, with gloved hands.

I had a fine old aunt who though perfectly *compos mentis* wouldn't drive with me at the wheel, she would only go with Plaste. I once had to make Plaste drive my car, because we all had to go to some funeral. I watched his methods. Plaste started almost ridiculously slowly, while my aunt sat on the edge of the seat leaning forward and bracing herself as if she were on a scenic railway. Then Plaste said slowly, "I hope you're not going to ask me to drive fast". A moment later my aunt said: "Thank goodness you're not one of those scorchers." Plaste answered quietly: "Can't afford to be, with all these Sunday School drivers about." This meant nothing at all, as far as I could see. But the black flowers in Aunt's hat wobbled. She was laughing. Plaste waved on a van packed with full milk-bottles. "See that fellow?" he said (the speedometer said eighteen), "though I expect you like to move a bit when the road's clear, you old serpent!" "Oh, if it's safe," Aunt said, pursing up her mouth and then suddenly smiling. "So long as I'm with a good driver."

Quite soon Plaste was taking bends at fifty and once passed a car on a corner, typical mistake. Immediately he was explaining to Aunt the danger of passing on a

104

corner, and she sat back relaxed, smiling and nodding. When his speed made it necessary for him to brake sharply he would always say "*Wow*—did you see that fellow?"

For more sophisticated passengers he would use different methods. For the boy who confuses good driving with good acceleration he would spend a lot of time, and make a good deal of noise, in second gear. With some people he found that a tremendous and to me quite ludicrous amount of hand-signalling created a good impression. Plaste had an instinct for this type, and would play up. With others, the lightly spoken technical word was a success, which reminds me that even in his little smashes, and he was by no means accident-free, Godfrey hardly ever lost face.[1] For instance I have known him, three times

[1] With accidents generally we have gone I think beyond the primitive rules which advised the basic techniques (i) to start shouting first (ii) to take out a notebook and write, saying nothing. As we have never been personally involved yet in any contretemps where any words of our prepared repartee have been of the slightest use or even heard, let me quote (because I admire them and because I want to say something positive) remarks made to me by a foreigner as he got out of his car to greet me, having run lightly into my side from a by-road when my car was stationary, outside the Sweet Nell & Co. Lipstick factory on the Great West Road. He simply smiled and said, "Well, it eez good? There are no corpse?" I was much struck with the untutored skill. It may be the basis of a new school.

running, stopped by lights, mistake reverse for first gear when moving forward on green. The third time he bumped back quite hard into the car which had been following him, and when the driver came round to expostulate, he said: "You realise what's happened of course. The malden rod must have leapt its pressure rim. One is helpless, I'm afraid. Look—can you give me a hand?" It may interest Maida readers to know that Plaste now lives not very far from Acacia Road, N.W.

2. FURTHER NOTES ON PIPE PLAY

Is Pipemanship on the decline? There is no doubt that this subject is profoundly historical. I think it is true to say that except with men in remote country rectories, boys between the age of eight and fifteen, the *nouveau feudal*, and a few somewhat older girls, the pipe in 1958 fails to impress.

Lifemanship's earlier annals record that we used to do a good deal of work, some of it published, on the use of the pipe in its role of Silent Conversationalist. If a young man wants to describe to you exactly why it is that he is totally unable to work, or a young girl wants to tell you how happy she is because she is in love with someone else, who is in love with someone else, it is useful, it may be essential, to have a pipe in your hand, and, if possible, smoke it. To look, during a pause, very hard at the mouthpiece, turning the pipe upside down. And we have explained how the prolonged bubbling blow through the stem of a rather wet pipe can give the effect not only that you are deeply sympathetic but are absolutely clear on the right course to pursue.

In addition to this tried basic, there are lesser uses of the pipe as a spreader of dis-ease.[1] At a party of the dinner-jacket order, for instance, the technique is to come not in a dinner jacket but in tails, rather loosely worn, and then as soon as possible put a pipe with a very large bowl and a very short stem in your mouth. Place your hands in your pockets, and walk slowly up and down on the outskirts. This suggests that there is not much difference to you between tails and bedroom slippers and that dressing up is absurd anyhow and that you are not going to be influenced by it.

The main complaint of women against pipes is that the pipe personality is boring and produces boredom. A rather confusing counter-effect can occasionally be made, therefore, by unpipelike people with an unpipelike pipe, small and straight, held horizontally in the mouth while speaking, in this strained position, quickly and wittily, yet with a certain amount of temperament and moodiness.

In spite of the great cigarette scare, only the most brilliant and advanced pipeman can succeed with the suggestion that the pipe is a symbol of Health, that the going for a walk with a pipe is as natural as,

[1] A good modern approach, if asked whether you are really a pipe-smoker, is to say that you have been asked to do so by the British Medical Association as a control. This means that somebody exactly the same as you is smoking cigarettes, which are known to be more harmful. By this means it is proved that they are more harmful.

and difficult to distinguish from, going for a walk with a dog. But indoors, controlled practised pipe smoking is capable of making a cigarette smoker seem flustered and untidy, particularly if the cigarette smoker is ashy and scruffy, can never laugh for fear of coughing, and maintains a long worm of ash messily drooping from his cigarette.[1]

Possible Slips

These may be serious. We ourselves have made mistakes. Early in life I made the primal pipe-fumble. Ostensibly to ask his advice, in reality to impress him with my talents, I called on a celebrated pipe-smoking author. I thought it would be a good thing if I myself had a pipe. After an hour's practice, I fancied I was perfect. It is not necessary to add that after a few minutes of my spitting and prodding and pecking, he asked me if I would like a cigarette, eventually (after much irritated difficulty) finding one for me at the bottom of his wife's handbag—a Turk, tasting of Valse Bleu, a medium-priced scent of the period.

Remember, always, that it is a grave mistake for the insignificant-looking man of no personality to buy a documentary film-producer's outfit and go about in sea boots, coarsely cut macintosh, no hat and huge carved pipes sticking out of the mouth and pockets like candelabra. If your personality is small,

---

[1] The best defence from the unkindness of being called "a cigaretty old thing" is to have a good deal of cigarette-holder work and plenty of crisp clicking and exact handling about your method of smoking them. It is not enough simply not to dribble.

be small in a delicate way and use, for instance, unusually thin cigarettes and tiny lighters.

Long practice and deep knowledge is the key to successful pipe control.

If you are going to possess a pipe, you must have the accoutrements and side effects which include, for instance, massive matches, and raw slices of unusual vegetables to preserve humidity in the pouch. If you are a pipe-is-my-best-friend man, it is advisable to study pipes as if they were pieces of rare porcelain, and know about pipe history. A sound gambit here is to show that everything is ever so much more early than anybody thought. So far, for instance, from Raleigh having introduced the primitive leaf to England, it is no exaggeration to say that what he brought back was in everything, perhaps, but the exact name and appearance, a packet of *Camels*. Try referring to neolithic times, mention Orkney excavations, and say something of the *Cigarro* casts of the mesolithic boulder and delta folk.

*   *   *

Tomorrow, at noon, in spite of the fact that they have been proved to kill you more quickly, I shall give up cigs and shall be once more slowly and carefully preparing the pipe which is going to be my friend, and watch the miniature wilderness of delicate tobacco fronds at the top of the bowl rot and moulder as they always do when I smoke them, to a damp and sticky block of seaweed.

V

PLOYS IN PROGRESS

Our purpose in this chapter is twofold. Its first object is to give some impression of the continuity, the multiplicity, and the ubiquity of liferesearch and lifecontributions. Its second is to give encouragement to those many workers, by sea and land, who have contributed their own ploy or ploylet, and passed it on to Yeovil, where, after vetting and polishing, we establish it as something of our own, occasionally mentioning the actual author in a footnote.

1. AIRCRAFT PASSENGERCRAFT
F. Wilson, Nettlebed

F. Wilson, basic collaborator in and illustrator of Gameslife, has a circle of admirers only less wide than that of the Founder. Holding a high place in the hierarchy (Nettlebed 2a) he is most generally known for the gambit in which he so majestically majors— the Secret Mission, which takes him to Singapore for tea and Beirut for elevenses. It should not be publicly revealed that secret mission is cover for private research: the reader must guess to what extent the development of certain ployfields owes its origin to the unconscious collaboration of H.M. Govt.

How to be top passenger is one of Wilson's flight

studies. Although genuinely V.I.P., he has found it necessary, owing to the intermittent failure of a somewhat fluctuating personality, to establish this fact. Here are some of his recommendations. Only the grammar, punctuation, and vocabulary have been altered by us.

1. Sometimes the most obvious is the most effective. On the walk across the tarmac, lean for support on the air hostess who has come to take over. The quiet word "Invalid" will be heard. A seat, perhaps even two, will be found for you away from the engine, near the air hostess, and right opposite the entrance to the bar. Remember to walk up steps one at a time. Many passengers will feel uneasy, and a few will think they have a Jonah on board. Murmurs of "Captain Ahab".

2. Once the best seat has been secured, invalid atmosphere can be dropped. During take-off, if novice air traveller in next seat is a little tense, mark correct approach by quietly relaxed attitude. Keep on right-hand glove and start reading. (Suggestions: Proust translated into Spanish—"much funnier": or take out a few wreaths of newspaper cuttings and say "Do you ever *read* your newspaper cuttings?—rather amusing.") If novice stares in

As soon as aircraft is well over ocean, Odoreida goes through the motions, with his arms, of the breast-stroke.

strained way at airstrip offer him the piece of barley sugar you have been given.[1]

3. When plane begins to sway in bumpy patch, say: "I *thought* I noticed a change in note and a momentary splutter. Have you ever thought how sensitive these vast flying machines are—how human, like you and me? Almost a comfort to know that they, too, can err." This is an Odoreida speciality. During the demonstration by air hostess, of Life Jacket drill, Odoreida always says: "I bet the rubber's perished."

2. The light put-off, or Club Stabiliser
Staff, London

Armstrong Walter was in our Club, the Sequoia. He was better dressed than myself, and his luncheon guest was better dressed than either of us. This

[1] Beware of possible counters. "Novice" may be Lifeman who says (a) "Take-off still gives me a kick . . . the sense of uncoiling energy . . ." Or (b) "An airfield is the place to see partridges. At Praha last month, I saw 7½ brace, plus four hares and six leverets."

would not do, so I said to him while walking to the bar: "Extremely sorry I couldn't get to your party the other day. I meant to write you a note. I didn't get away from my meeting till nearly midnight."

As A.W. has never asked me to a party, and almost certainly has never thought of doing so, this microscopically *broke flow*, or at any rate led to explanations *which I could hurry apologetically away from*.

3. "Dont's Let's Have too much Christian-naming"
Staff

Here is a crisp lifeplay, and this is its sequence. For years Mr. Black has been calling Mr. White "White"—i.e. by his surname. Then one day he, Black, on some relaxed occasion, will call White "Arthur". This is a trap. White, encouraged by this, will call Black "Nevill" next time he meets him. This is what Black has been waiting for. He instantly calls White "White" like a sledge-hammer, repeating this with a strong suggestion of reproof, and more than a hint that he for one is not going to indulge in a forced matiness reminiscent of the Light Programme.

4. Let Me Read Your Hands
J. Bryan III, Florida

Last week in Florida, I had an evening with Robert Frost. The conversation turned to fortune telling, and he told me about a hostess who insisted

s.—8   113

that Mrs. S. read his palm: "My dear, she's too marvellous and everything she tells you . . . well!" Mrs.
S. was eager to read the great poet's palm, so he held
it out, first right then left. She bent over it, scrutinised
it with knotted brows. Then shoving his hand aside,
said "Sorry, but I'm all out of practice," and walked
off. Frost says that ever since, when he walks down
the street, he looks over his shoulder.

5. Christmas Feeling
G. Odoreida, Yeovil

Odoreida sends as Christmas card a twopenny post-
card of Llandudno railway station with "My. Xmas
from Mr. & Mrs. G. Odoreida" stamped on in mauve
ink, the ink very faint and the stamp much worn.

6. When to Use Thin Spidery Handwriting
J. Bryan III

Yesterday, I stopped in to see a friend of mine,
and parked my car beside B's house, just in front of
a gate marked DO NOT BLOCK THIS DRIVEWAY.
I knew that it really wasn't a driveway at all, but
B's system of reserving a parking space for himself.
When my visit ended, I found a note on the seat
of my car, "Please do not block my driveway again.
E. B." (This was B's wife.) So I borrowed some
stationery from a friend of mine named Buffington
(a perfect name for this ploy), persuaded a lady with
a spidery handwriting to follow my copy, and sent
this letter.

Sir:

I was carrying some jelly to an *invalid* in your neighbourhood yesterday morning, and since my hip does not permit me to walk more than a few yards, I parked my car nearby, in front of what turned out to be *your* house. Only then did I notice your sign, *ordering* the *public* to stay away! I rang your doorbell, to *beg* five minutes of *grace*, and waited and waited, but *no one* answered. My hip was beginning to pain me, so I *peeked* through your gate and discovered that your "driveway" (!) was nothing more than a *narrow walk*, impassable by any vehicle wider than a child's *express wagon* or "*Irish mail*"! You should be *ashamed* of yourself for trying to label this *path* a *driveway*! I propose to park there *whenever* I wish, and I would welcome an opportunity to defend my *right* to do so in a court of law.

My uncle, the late Major Wyndham Buffington, *died* for his convictions, on the bloody field of Sharpsburg. If necessary, *I* am prepared to do *no less.*

I remain, Sir,

(Miss) SALLY LOU BUFFINGTON

P.S. I would have communicated with you *at once*, but this experience upset me so that my doctor made me spend yesterday afternoon with the *blinds drawn*!

VI

SUPERYULE

How to be Top Christmas

LET US FIRST DEFINE the Basic Christmas Gambit.
It is: to seem to be more truly Christmas than other
people; to be top man, for geniality; to be one up in
general Christmas kindliness; to be so managingly
unobtrusive in the background that background
becomes foreground.

Our early work on this subject, some of it published, may now look primitive and formless, but it
was basically sound. It was constructed, students
may remember, on the teaching of Arthur Meriton,
chosen for his fine Christmas name, and developed
by him as Good Old Uncle Arthurship. He was
expert in inducing a suggestion that he was Top
Uncle at Christmas Parties. If he found children
disliked his hearty voice, and they often loathed it,
he would immediately switch to an extremely quiet
tone, crouch down on his knees so that his face was
dead level with that of the smallest child in the room,
speak to it so quietly and naturally as to be in-
audible, and thereby achieve a kind of one-upness.
Being nice to the smallest child present is unassailably
correct Christmas play. Speaking to children absolutely naturally impresses grown ups; and Meriton

made a speciality of this. If the child started to scream, Meriton used to say, "Somebody's been made to feel a little out of it lately, haven't they?" as if it was somebody else's fault.

This sort of thing was rather in Meriton's family. He had a brother, Sebastian, who created a great Christmas reputation for himself by specialising in one ploy, and one only, which we have listed as How to Make Parents Feel Awkward about whether they make their children believe in Santa Claus.

To Santa-Claus-is-Real parents Sebastian would say: "You let them believe?"

PARENT: Sort of.

SEB: And then, later, when they find out the truth——

PARENT: Oh, well.

SEB: Do you realise that to Charlie you are a king, an emperor, a god who can do no wrong, much less suggest a falsehood?

PARENT: You mean . . . sort of . . . oh, I don't know.

SEB: A child's mind is like a new leaf, as perfect as a spring shoot. But the caterpillar is not far away.

I have heard Seb go on like this for five minutes and then trot off to the garden to challenge a Santa-Claus-is-*not*-real father and start on him like this.

SEB: Hygienic.

FATHER: I beg your pardon?

SEB: No nonsense about you, and "no such person as Santa Claus". Good luck to you.

FATHER: Well, thanks.

SEB: I was brought up in that tradition too—calm, rational, very modern pictures, food sterilised to the last drop.

FATHER: Oh, I don't know.

SEB: Of *course* Santa Claus is not real: and of *course* not one atom of romance, nor the warmth of make-believe, must stain the black and white of the mind of the child of the rationalist.

Pre-Christmas Technique

All this may be described as basic Christmas play. Recently we have been devoting more time to what we call Counter-Christmassing. In this the expert prepares his lifefield by taking the Christmas out of Christmas for other people before it starts. This is obviously sound lifemanship in general: in particular it makes it easier for the lifeman, by judicious timing, to be top geniality at the right moment.

"Thank Goodness That's Over"

Coad-Sanderson has always been my model here. He was in advertising, and to be in advertising is to be naturally one up on everything except perhaps advertising itself. It is impossible for an advertising man not to know the inside facts about anything essential which can conceivably be bought, like boots and electric toothbrushes, and a lot of things which can't conceivably be bought as well, like Christmas.

Coad's small pale face was so ordinary that it was

only just possible to distinguish him from other people by the small pale moustache, which seemed fixed by a tin-tack, as it were, in the middle of it. His face hadn't got a line on it because he didn't go in for expression, as he spent his life not reacting to anything in any way whatever, much less showing surprise. Round about the beginning of December, when we began to get a bit warmed up and prospective about Christmas, and started mentioning it, he would say:

"Well, thank God that's over."

"How do you mean?", we would say.

"Well, of course, this Christmas started for me in February."

"How February?"

"Frightful flare-up deciding on an entirely new lay-out for Shortt & Weitz's street level window-display for Christmas 1958. As you can imagine our client is on the conservative side. A tremendous robin-and-mistletoe man, but it wasn't until March that I convinced him that festooning them with holly wasn't the best way to sell ladies' girdles— indeed that it was definitely *Resistenz* advertising."

Coad made really an extremely good story of these Christmas advertising meetings, but of course it had a very sapping effect on the thrill of holly and mistletoe which normally we wouldn't have thought of till rather late, and suddenly, two days before Christmas. Round about May if you went to Coad's office for a drink, you would find him shouting down the telephone about colour ads behind schedule for the Christmas number. Commuting in America on some cool beach in Maine, he would be writing letters to a comic artist in Georgetown briefed to invent, during a humid spell in Washington D.C., a comic picture of a St. Bernard dog in a snowy frozen waste. In fact not only in his work but in his life Coad was an out-of-season man, so that one had the feeling that whatever week of the year was the actual week it was an out-of-date week so far as Coad was concerned, Christmas, of course, especially.

Office Partyship

Coad was brilliant in his way. But the nigglingness of Coad did limit his effectiveness, and just where you would expect an advertising man to shine he was not really at his best. I mean, of course, in the important Christmas activity of his partyship. The art of office Christmas Partyship is the art of taking the opportunity to get one up on your rivals at that very time when surely to goodness all ranks are level and all thoughts of self-promotion, and indeed any business thoughts of any kind whatever, at that one time of the year when everybody should be perfectly natural together, shall and must be in abeyance.

This of course is a great time for the go-ahead mid-ranking executive. Coad's ordinariness stood him in bad stead here as few people could remember who he was outside his office. What one wants here is the sitting-on-the-corner-of-the-table approach, one foot on the ground, listening extremely hard, smilingly but intently, to whatever anybody is saying to you. I must say dear old Gattling used to do very well here before he began to go bald in that curious way in which he went bald. These are his notes.

One must mix of course, said Gattling, but at the same time let it be seen that you are the one who even at the party keeps his essential finger on the remorseless pulse of business events and e.g. takes one or two squints at the tape machine.

Simultaneously, and connected with this, you must make use of the opportunity to show that you are in the secret confidence of the managing director by accidentally revealing, twice, that you are on much more familiar terms with him than your official ranking might suggest, and that you are much better at talking to him easily than Old W. who has been his Number Three for 22 years, and in fact you have only just got to take a glance at me, now, to observe that rather pleasant relationship which has grown up between me and the managing director, who really, in a way, regards me as a sort of son.

But above all Gattling did this tremendous mixing at the Party. He was extremely good too at being perfectly natural, without of course a trace of flirtation, to the two prettiest office secretaries simultaneously, and then at looking just as intently and interestedly at Miss Heason, who was easily the plainest woman in the building. Gattling would also amusingly take part in the fun, do good imitations of X and Y, but essentially kindly ones, and show that

GATTLING BEING RATHER WONDERFUL
with Junior Stenographer.

he was essentially more youthful than many younger members of the staff and that that helped him to understand them.

Finally, he was also able, and this needed great care, to show that he was the one who could thoroughly mix and yet never get in the least bit tight. If Gattling had a fault, it was that he sometimes overdid this business of demonstrating that he was not in the least bit tight, though sometimes, afterwards, Gattling did well by being "a tiny bit sorry that 'J. G.' rather overdid it at that party".

I would like to add this note of my own.

(1) If you are the mad-ideas man with a flair, it is O.K. to get pretty gay and mad: and it is possible in the midst of the party to have mad salesmanship

ideas and be brilliant about work to show how your real interests lie, revealed *in vino*.

(2) If you are the smart wife of director or chief executive, you must first find out what kind of clothes all the other women are going to be supposed to wear and then dress in the exact opposite manner. For instance, if the juniors are going to come low, be yourself buttoned up to the neck.

Not Being Sure About Dickens

My final example of advanced Christmas lifemanship I owe largely to the work of one woman, Angela Nethersole. The active part of her career belongs to a tremendously place-name-y village under the North Downs much visited by myself during Christmas holidays since the war.

Angela is neither pretty nor plain, but she is quite genuinely jolly, and likes fun; and she likes Christmas. Yet as soon as Angela is around at that time of year, one longs passionately for Christmas to be over, and nobody knows quite how she has done it.

One point she makes is that Christmas to be truly jolly must be spontaneous, and yet the way she says this is one of the most dampening things she does. She used to be very fond of Charles Dickens until she read the long life of him by Stebb-Nutting, which of course is very psycho and casts such a completely new light on *A Christmas Carol*. It was soon after this revelation that Angela began to be down on Christmassy Christmas cards. Last year she sent me a picture of the mummy of an ancient Christian found in Rome with "Via Appia" on it. This was obviously anti-Dickensy.

Near Christmas, Angela starts referring to the "Santa Claus figure". She says that about three-quarters of our Christmas customs are pagan, and that our own perfectly straightforward way of always putting stuffing in our turkey is Bronze Age, and that you still find it in the disembowelling rites of Bush culture.

I always like to play a few carols on the piano just about Christmas time, and I like it when other people join in, which is what generally happens. Gattling can put in quite a good bass to anything I play. But last year Angela Nethersole drifted in and almost at once I was conscious of a climatic change. Suddenly, while I was playing not untunefully, she said: "Don't you think those lovely carols sound much better unaccompanied?" Gattling agreed, like a fool. But in less than two minutes it was clear that what Angela really meant was that it was better if *she* were to be in charge of the singing. "It is a fifteenth century carol, 'Icycle holde thee strait'," she was saying in her extraordinarily clear voice, which seemed also to suggest that the spelling was funny. She then *took out a tuning fork, and struck it*, made two or three quick passes with her hands, and started to sing this tune with four other people who seemed suddenly to have appeared from nowhere. They must have been practising it for days; and perhaps the most annoying thing was the way they stood absolutely still for

THE "MUCH-BETTER-WITHOUT-AN-ACCOMPANIMENT" PLOY
IN ACTION.

pauses between verses. A lot of people sheepishly clapped.

Still there is no doubt that this one-up attitude to carols was a fine Christmas gambit, much better than such old-fashioned Christmas Day ploys as making the shyest and most nondescript member of the party dress up to take the part of Santa Claus, or, during the present-giving, making sure that you give Freddy exactly the same sort of present that Freddy gives you, but making it obvious, if it is given in public, that yours is the better quality, or, if given in private, worse. Against the expert Christmas man there is no sure defence, and it is better to fall back on the general suggestion that all this being tremendously nice at Christmas is redolent of Somebody covering up a tendency to be tremendously nasty all the rest of the year. Suggest that for you, personally, it makes no difference. Say almost anything, because whatever you say, at this time of year especially, no one will pay any attention.

125

ENVOY

Now Superman says farewell—indeed Superman is already on the way to a new assignment. International Lifemanship has enlisted his services: counter-Marxmanship absorbs his waning powers. His broadcast to the American nation on April 20th was badly jammed, but certain sentences were heard, a few phrases recorded:

. . . would start by saying that Lifemanship is exactly as old as the very words diplomacy and foreign policy. The utter unsuitability of the term "foreign policy" in the context of friendship between people—what a fine gambit in itself. And the root meaning of diplomacy is of course "double"— diplous, duplicity . . .

Khrushchev says, "Let us end atomic experiment". Think for a moment of historical Summit ploys. No need to remind you of Trojan Horsemanship, which perfectly describes the basic Khrushchev gambit. It is a type of all the doubleness of diplomacy. In the very act of making a friendly gesture—you can see the European headlines (GENEROUS GESTURE BY GREEK GOVERNMENT) and the attack is already starting . . .

. . . notice the splendid lifeword of the Greeks— they were *liberating* Helen of Troy.

. . . the perpetual one-upness of Marxmanship . . .

that the Suez incident occupied five times the space of the Hungarian massacre when the United Nations met to register moral disapproval. One-downness by nature . . . of Eden.

Why is the one-upness of Khrushchev always intact? Is it an example of Beyond the Palemanship, which can use the very words "we have no further territorial ambitions" as the code phrase for an unprovoked attack? . . .

Brinkmanship is a clever way of describing the Dulles attitude: but like all Americans, through some fatal streak of reasonableness or human feeling he falls short as complete International Lifeman.[1] Khrushchev is the true Brinkman: his existence depending, as Russian rule has depended for thirty years, on enemy-at-the-gatemanship . . . diverting attention from the making of lethal weapons by sidelines made to please the public . . . the satellite gambit or Sputnik ploy. This is part of National Geophysical Yearmanship, and typically Marxian.

But Khrushchev must always be one-up because he is more words-of-one-syllable. "End the bomb" can be understood by three-quarters of the world: "Organise a committee for international inspection and mutual restraint" can only be understood by less than one-twentieth of it. "Summit Conference" is easy to understand: "Exploratory committees to

[1] Occasionally the U.S. Government can deliver itself of a basic lifespeech, made for instance by Eisenhower more effective by the fact that he believes it himself. It was at the time of Suez that we heard him say: "America has no financial ambitions in the Middle East."

ensure that a conference is effective" is a one-down phrase because it needs thought to understand what it means.

In the words of R. Abernethy, International Lifemanship is lifemanship carried to a point which stops short only at deathmanship, or the art of winning the world without actually blowing it up. (*The rest of the discourse was lost in a succession of buzzes and pings.*)

"A HELPING HAND"